THE
MALTESE

ANNA KATHERINE NICHOLAS

Title page photo: Ch. So Big's Desert Delight, owned by Mrs. Freda Tinsley, Rebecca's Maltese, Scottsdale, Arizona.

ISBN 0-87666-569-5

Distributed in the UNITED STATES by T.F.H. Publications, Inc., 211 West Sylvania Avenue, Neptune City, NJ 07753; in CANADA by H & L Pet Supplies Inc., 27 Kingston Crescent, Kitchener, Ontario N2B 2T6; Rolf C. Hagen Ltd., 3225 Sartelon Street, Montreal 382 Quebec; in ENGLAND by T.F.H. Publications Limited, 4 Kier Park, Ascot, Berkshire SL5 7DS; in AUSTRALIA AND THE SOUTH PACIFIC by T.F.H. (Australia) Pty. Ltd., Box 149, Brookvale 2100 N.S.W., Australia; in NEW ZEALAND by Ross Haines & Son, Ltd., 18 Monmouth Street, Grey Lynn, Auckland 2 New Zealand; in SINGAPORE AND MALAYSIA by MPH Distributors Pte., 71-77 Stamford Road, Singapore 0617; in the PHILIPPINES by Bio-Research, 5 Lippay Street, San Lorenzo Village, Makati, Rizal; in SOUTH AFRICA by Multipet Pty. Ltd., 30 Turners Avenue, Durban 4001. Published by T.F.H. Publications Inc., Ltd., the British Crown Colony of Hong Kong.

Dedication

To all of the beautiful Maltese I have admired in the judging ring over the years, with a special bow to Champion Musi of Villa Malta, the first of his breed to win a Best in Show from me.

In Appreciation

Writing this book has been a very pleasant task, filled with nostalgia in many cases as I have looked back over the years and remembered dogs and people who have contributed toward the success which the Maltese has met.

The Maltese Fancy has been most generous in its cooperation with my efforts. To everyone who has helped by loaning pictures for this book, I thank you. Also my gratitude is extended to those who have submitted kennel histories on their dogs and other important information on the breed. They have done much to add interest to our content and therefore are sincerely appreciated.

A special thanks to Mrs. Anna Mae Hardy, owner of the Russ Ann Maltese, for her excellent advice on coat care and grooming which has formed the basis of my chapter covering these subjects. Her gracious willingness to help, and permission to use her findings on how to keep the coat of your Maltese at its best, have added up to a description of coat care all should be able to follow. Mrs. Hardy is a lady who learned how to do it herself the hard way—by the trial and error method—so well that she has put a famed Best in Show winner into the ring successfully. Our gratitude is sincere to her for sharing her grooming techniques with our readers.

Gail Hennessey had just returned from visiting Crufts when we asked her for some notes on what she had seen in the Maltese world there. She has shared the excitement of Crufts with us, helping to make our chapter on Maltese activities in Great Britain right up to the moment, along with some information about the Maltese Club in Great Britain and some of the dogs she admired.

Marcia Foy, as always, has been on the job reading copy and helping to get everything co-ordinated.

Thank you, one and all! I hope that the Maltese Fancy will derive as much pleasure from the completed book as I have had from the hours spent working on it, telling of a breed I have long loved.

Anna Katherine Nicholas.

Contents

About the Author

Since early childhood, Anna Katherine Nicholas has been involved with dogs. Her first pets were a Boston Terrier, an Airedale, and a German Shepherd. Then, in 1925, came the first of the Pekingese—a gift from a friend who raised them. Now her home is shared with a Miniature Poodle and a dozen or so Beagles, including her noted Best in Show dog and National Specialty winner, Champion Rockaplenty's Wild Oats, a Gold Certificate sire (one of the breed's truly great stud dogs), who as a show dog was Top Beagle in the Nation in 1973. She also owns Champion Foyscroft True Blue Lou, Foyscroft Aces Are Wild, and in co-ownership with Marcia Foy, who lives with her, Champion Foyscroft Triple Mitey Migit.

Miss Nicholas is best known throughout the Dog Fancy as a writer and as a judge. Her first magazine article, published in *Dog News* magazine around 1930, was about Pekingese; and this was followed by a widely acclaimed breed column, "Peeking at the Pekingese" which appeared for at least two decades, originally in *Dogdom*, then, following the demise of that publication, in *Popular Dogs*. During the 1940's she was Boxer columnist for *Pure-Bred Dogs, American Kennel Gazette* and for *Boxer Briefs*. More recently many of her articles, geared to interest fanciers of every breed, have appeared in *Popular Dogs, Pure-Bred Dogs, American Kennel Gazette, Show Dogs, Dog Fancy,* and *The World of the Working Dog*. Currently she is a featured regular columnist in *Kennel Review, Dog World, Canine Chronicle* and *The Dog Fancier* (Canadian). Her *Dog World* column, "Here, There and Everywhere," was the Dog Writers Association of America winner of the Best Series in a Dog Magazine Award for 1979.

It was during the late 1930's that Miss Nicholas' first book, *The Pekingese*, appeared, published by and written at the request of the Judy Publishing Company. This book completely sold out and is now a collector's item, as is her *The Skye Terrier Book*, which was published by the Skye Terrier Club of America during the early 1960's.

In 1970 Miss Nicholas won the Dog Writers Association of America award for the Best Technical Book of the Year with her *Nicholas Guide to Dog Judging*, published by Howell Book House. In 1979 the revision of this book again won the Dog Writers Association of America Best Technical Book Award, the first time ever that a revision has been so honored by this association.

In the early 1970's, Miss Nicholas co-authored, with Joan Brearley, five breed books which were published by T.F.H. Publications, Inc. These were *This is the Bichon Frise, The Wonderful World of Beagles and Beagling* (winner of a Dog Writers Association of America Honorable Mention Award), *The Book of the Pekingese, The Book of the Boxer,* and *This is the Skye Terrier.*

During recent years, Miss Nicholas has been writing books consistently for T.F.H. These include *Successful Dog Show Exhibiting, The Book of the Rottweiler, The Book of the Poodle, The Book of the Labrador Retriever, The Book of the English Springer Spaniel, The Book of the Golden Retriever,* and *The Book of the German Shepherd Dog.* Currently she is working on *The Book of the Shetland Sheepdog,* which will be another breed spectacular, and in the same series with the one you are now reading, *This is the Chow Chow, This is the Keeshond, This is the Cocker Spaniel,* and several additional titles. In the T.F.H. "KW" series, she has done *Rottweilers, Weimaraners* and *Norwegian Elkhounds.* She has also supplied the American chapters for two English publications, imported by T.F.H. *The Staffordshire Bull Terrier* and *The Jack Russell Terrier.*

Miss Nicholas, in addition to her four Dog Writers Association of America awards, has on two occasions been honored with the *Kennel Review* "Winkie" as Dog Writer of the Year; and in both 1977 and 1982 she was recipient of the Gaines "Fido" award as Journalist of the Year in Dogs.

Her judging career began in 1934 at the First Company Governors' Foot Guard in Hartford, Connecticut, drawing the largest Pekingese entry ever assembled to date at this event. Presently she is approved to judge all Hounds, Terriers, Toys, and Non-Sporting Dogs; all Pointers, English and Gordon Setters, Vizslas, Weimaraners and Wire-haired Pointing Griffons in Sporting breeds and, in Working Group, Boxers and Doberman Pinschers. In 1970 she became the third woman in history to judge Best in Show at the prestigious Westminster Kennel Club

The fabulous Ch. Musi of Villa Malta, one of the earliest consistent Best in Show Maltese, with breeder-owner-handler Dr. Vincenzo Calvaresi taking Best in Show at Longshore-Southport Kennel Club in 1959, Anna Katherine Nicholas judge.

Dog Show, where she has officiated on some sixteen other occasions through the years. In addition to her numerous Westminster assignments, Miss Nicholas has judged at such other outstandingly important events as Santa Barbara, Trenton, Chicago International, the Sportsmans in Canada, the Metropolitan in Canada, and Specialty Shows in several dozen breeds both in the United States and in Canada. She has judged in almost every one of the mainland United States and in four Canadian provinces, and her services are constantly sought in other countries.

Through the years, Miss Nicholas has held important offices in a great many all-breed and Specialty clubs. She still remains an honorary member of several of them.

Eng. Ch. Harlingen Snowman, a prominent winner and important sire, was bred by Miss M. van Oppen and born in 1926 and became a champion in 1927.

Chapter I
Origin and Early History
of the Maltese

That the Maltese is a breed of dog whose roots go far back into antiquity and that these dogs are native to the Mediterranean area are statements on which historians agree. From there, however, a question has been raised as to whether these dogs were in truth actually first seen on the Island of Malta, as is most widely accepted; or whether Melita, a town in Sicily, was the breed's true birthplace. Both theories have been advanced, and both would seem to have strong factual evidence behind them.

The historian, Strabo (25 A.D.) wrote and is quoted as having stated: "There is a town in Sicily called Melita whence are exported many beautiful dogs called Canis Melitei." These words give credence to the theory that perhaps the breed did originate there. On the other hand, the far more popular belief is that Malta was the true birthplace of those little dogs, a belief so strong that for years they have been referred to as "Ye Ancient Dogge of Malta." Substantiating this point of view are the words of a poet, Marcus Valerius Martialis (popularly known as Martial, born in 38 A.D., thirteen years prior to the aforementioned historian, Strabo) in praise of a Maltese owned by Publius, the Roman Governor of Malta, this little dog obviously having been personally known to Martial. There is a possibility both ways here, we feel. Perhaps the original dogs *did* go to Malta by way of Sicily—or vice versa. Or perhaps they were established in both places at about the same time. Who can say as a certainty when so many centuries have elapsed? One thing is absolutely correct, from all we have read. Whichever way it began, the ancestors of our little Maltese of the present day enjoyed tremendous favor and popularity on the Island of Malta, where they were loved and valued as pets by the aristocracy. From the very beginning,

Maltese have appealed to people of taste and refinement, who appreciate the beauty and personality of such vivacious, loving, tiny, and sturdy little dogs. The changes in the breed so far as appearance and character are concerned have been slight, indeed, throughout the ages.

Throughout the ancient Mediterranean world, the Maltese dogs were treasured and esteemed. The Greeks were especially appreciative of them, as noted in paintings and ceramic art from early times, and were known to erect tombs in their memory. We have heard of an easily recognizable and lovely Maltese dog's likeness depicted on a vase found at Vulci which formed a part of the famed Bassegio collection. The strong probability exists that Maltese dogs were worshipped by the Egyptians, as it has been written that a very good model of one was unearthed in the Fayum in Egypt.

We have already referred to the poet Martial's tribute to the Maltese owned by Publius, the Governor of Malta. This little dog was named Issa, and Martial wrote as follows: "Issa is more frolicsome than Catulla's sparrow. Issa is purer than a dove's kiss. Issa is gentler than a maiden. Issa is more precious than Indian gems. Lest the last days that she sees light should snatch her from him forever, Publius has had her picture painted—". The portrait, we understand, is so true to life as to be barely distinguishable from the actual dog.

Obviously, little dogs of such charm and beauty became popular subjects with the poets and with great portrait painters. Callimachus the Elder (384-322 B.C.), Pliny the Elder (23 B.C.—79 A.D.), and Saint Clement of Alexandria are among those who paid word tribute to them.

Maltese were eagerly accepted by the British aristocracy, so well known for their love of dogs, and from the time of Queen Elizabeth I frequent mention of them has appeared in British literature and they have been immortalized by famous artists there as in their earlier days. Queen Elizabeth's personal physician, Dr. Johannus Caius, is one of the most respected and frequently quoted canine historians of all times. The following are his comments on the Maltese:

> There is among us another kind of highbred dog, but outside the common run of these dogs, Callimachus called [them] Melitei from the Island of Malta. That kind is *very*

small indeed, and chiefly sought after for the pleasure and amusement of women. The smaller the kind, the more pleasing it is; so that they may carry them in their bosoms, in their beds, and in their arms while in their carriages.

It is interesting to note the emphasis on smallness of size which right from the very beginning has been placed on these little dogs, descriptions of which have ranged at varying times from "the size of squirrels" to "not bigger than the common ferret." Perhaps particular thought should be given to this fact by present-day breeders and judges, for while we have many exquisite Maltese of correct size in our show rings, there is also a tendency toward increased size to be noted among some in the United States.

Among admired and famous paintings which feature or include Maltese from the days of their early popularity in Great Britain we find one called "Railway Station," painted by W. Powell Frith, R.A., of an elderly lady holding a Maltese in her arms. A portrait of Nellie O'Brien, done in 1763 by Sir Joshua Reynolds, features a quite handsome Maltese along with the principal subject. And of course there is the famous Sir Edwin Landseer portrait of a Maltese entitled, rather inaccurately, "The Last of the Race," done in 1840 when the little dogs had become, temporarily, quite scarce there. Happily this was a very short-lived situation, as those who loved and were interested in carrying on the breed imported several from Malta, which we understand formed the basic stock for the later generations of Maltese in England.

At one period in their history, Maltese were known as Maltese Terriers, which has since been proven incorrect. The Maltese is actually of *spaniel* descent, and the Terrier misnomer no doubt came about through the breed's courageous terrier-like attitude.

Irish Ch. Rahara Starbound, Top Winning Maltese in Ireland for 1982. Owner, Mr. J. K. Salisbury, Bellebane Maltese, North Wales. Photo at age 20 months.

Chapter II
Maltese in England
and Other Countries

From the very beginning of dog shows in Great Britain, Maltese were shown with regularity, their popularity growing steadily from the 1850's until the beginning of World War I. Then, as with many other breeds, they suffered a setback. However, this was only temporary, and with the end of the war Maltese fanciers quickly started selecting new breeding stock to intermix with their own. Interestingly, one of the important producers of this period, which we have read described as "a very fine small bitch" was Harlingen Dolly, one of several imported from Holland and Germany, which when bred to the English dogs had a highly beneficial influence on future generations of the breed. It is said that the majority of Maltese in Great Britain during the 1930's could be traced back to at least partial Dutch and German ancestry.

Anyone even slightly familiar with pure-bred dogs in Great Britain during her lifetime and reign must be aware of Queen Victoria's tremendous interest in and love for dogs. She was an ardent enthusiast who owned many breeds and also one who enjoyed the competition of dog shows. Maltese, I am sure, must have won her heart on sight! She was, of course, an owner of the breed.

In fact we have read a story about a couple named Mr. and Mrs. Lukey who discovered during their travels in Manila a pair of Maltese which they purchased at considerable expense to present as a gift to Her Majesty. They did not realize that the coats would need care during the long voyage to England; thus, when the Lukeys saw the dogs upon arrival, they were so shocked at the results of nine months' neglect that they were embarrassed to take them to the Queen, so they were never presented. All was

15

not lost, so the story goes, as the pair were bred from and proved to be excellent producers, their offspring being progenitors of later Maltese both in England and in the United States.

Prior to World War I, England's outstanding Maltese was probably Champion Snowcloud of Esperence, whose coat we understand measured twenty-one inches across the back and sides. Champion Snowcloud was owned by Mrs. Horowitz.

Post-war breeders of Maltese in England included Miss M. van Oppen who bred, among others, Champion Harlingen Snowman, born in 1926, who won four Challenge Certificates and became a champion during the following year. Snowman sired Champion Harlingen Emblem (from Harlingen Miracle) who won a first Certificate at the Kennel Club Show in 1931, finishing title shortly thereafter. Snowman also sired Champion White Chick, bred and owned by Mrs. L. H. Card, another consistent winner of the early and mid-1930's.

Miss M. Neame's Maltese were famous winners of this period and included Champion Invicta Meadowsweet, Champion Invicta Urania, Champion Invicta Fido, and Champion Invicta Quip. Miss M. Shepperd had the Maltessas, also including some splendid winners. And Achmonie dogs, too, were among the nicest.

The Maltese Club of Great Britain was founded on December 8th 1934, thus the Club will be having a Golden Jubilee Celebration on December 8th 1984, honoring their first fifty years. We wish them many happy returns! It was not until April 16th 1966 that the Maltese Club of Great Britain's first Championship Show was held in London. The officiating judges were Mrs. Brierley, owner of Leckhampton Maltese, and Miss Wild of Cosvale Maltese. Mrs. Brierley judged dogs at this 1966 event; Miss Wild judged the bitches. Ms. B. Worthington served as referee for this first Championship Show and will be returning as the officiating judge for the Jubilee Show.

It is interesting to look back and find that the entry for this first Maltese Club Championship Show numbered forty-six dogs in a total entry of 109. Mrs. T. Kirl's Immacula Top-O-Pole took the dog Challenge Certificate (his second) from the Junior Class. Mrs. Darcey's Triogen Toppet came away with the Bitch Challenge Certificate, Best in Show, and a brand new title of "champion." The reserves, both of whom also gained championship titles in the near future, were Mrs. Lewin's Ellwin's Pipello in dogs and Mrs. White's Vicbretta Rhapsody in bitches. Best puppy was Vicbretta Genevive.

Plans for the Golden Jubilee gala are enormously exciting. Twenty-three silver cups will be presented to the winners, along with shields and rosettes, and there will be twenty classes in which to compete. 1984 should be a banner year in the British Maltese world! There will be stands with Maltese memorabilia on display (the Maltese folks are among the most avid collectors of anything depicting their breed), and there will be a lovely gallery of past champions. It seems very probable that 1982's banner turnout, consisting of fifty-nine dogs in 144 entries, will be very handily surpassed!

On the present-day dog show scene in England, one finds some very outstanding and very dedicated Maltese breeders who are producing Maltese of quality and merit. Among the most successful of these are Mr. and Mrs. David Herrieff, whose dogs are now in their sixth homebred generation, who in 1983 had the honor of winning the Toy Group at Crufts, which is Great Britain's most prestigious dog show, with their Champion Snowgoose Valient Lad, known to his admiring friends as "Benjamin." The previous year this fine little dog had won all his classes plus the dog Challenge Certificate and Best in Show; and he had also won Best in Show at the South Eastern Toy Dog Show, where he gained the dog Challenge Certificate, too. Thus the Crufts Challenge Certificate was his third, making him a champion in about as nice a manner as could be imagined.

Valient Lad was one of two puppies in his litter, and although primarily interested more in breeding than in showing, Mrs. Herrieff saw his quality immediately and thus was anxious to get him out in competition. He has certainly done her proud! Also he is reproducing his quality in his puppies, two of which, Movalian Sugar Puff and Snowgoose Yousel of Anna Marie, won all of their classes at Crufts.

Gosmore Maltese, owned by Mrs. Audrey Dallison, are part of one of the top kennels in Great Britain since World War II, where many breeds of dog have been raised and many records broken. In the early 1970's Mrs. Dallison gave up her actual kennels, moving to her present location at Gerrards Cross in Bucks, deciding then to concentrate only on Maltese. Her reason was that she was finding it difficult to combine a steadily growing

The magnificent Eng. Ch. Snowgoose Valient Lad, bred, owned and handled by Mrs. Vicki Herrieff to Best Toy at Crufts in 1983.

Eng. Ch. Gosmore Le Petit Chanteur, by Eng. Ch. Shenala Hamish ex Eng. Ch. Elwin Petite Chanteuse is among the outstanding Maltese at England's famed Gosmore Kennels, Mrs. A. Dallison, Gerrards Cross, Bucks.

Eng. Ch. Gosmore Tobias at 10 weeks. One of the outstanding winners sired by Eng. Ch. Gosmore Vicbrita Tristan, owned by Mrs. A. Dallison, Gerrards Cross, Bucks, England.

An important Maltese of the early 1930s, Eng. Ch. Harlingen Emblem, by Eng. Ch. Harlingen Snowman ex Eng. Ch. Harlingen Miracle, was bred by Mrs. M. Roberts and born in 1930.

successful judging career with owning top winning dogs. Since Maltese were her favorites, she decided to specialize in them and only to campaign dogs to their titles. She endeavors to limit the number of dogs she keeps to roughly a dozen, including puppies, all of which live in the house with her and for which she cares personally, except when away either judging or exhibiting.

Mrs. Dallison is following her original breeding program in Maltese, which is very close line-breeding based principally on Vicbrita, which she considered the top English Maltese kennel of its day and which unfortunately is no longer active. She has been most successful in combining the Vicbrita line with Shenala Hamish, a combination which has thrown winners in every litter.

Mrs. Dallison feels that Champion Gosmore Vicbrita Tristan has undoubtedly been one of the top sires because he has never been placed at public stud and over the years has been allowed for use only to a small number of outside bitches. He was top stud dog among British Maltese over several years, but since moving to her current location, Mrs. Dallison has not kept records. Her Champion Gosmore Le Petit Chanteur and Champion Gosmore Tobias she considers to be "the best that Tristan has yet produced." Two other young English dogs she mentions with admiration from other kennels are Champion Shenala Renoir and Champion Francoombe Star Turn. At the present time, Tobias (named for his grandsire, as right from the first he was an outstanding dog) is siring some exciting puppies which should help keep the Gosmore banner high in the future.

Two of Mrs. Dallison's Maltese, Gosmore Fairy Footsteps and Gosmore Tobias, scored for her the very admirable double victory of Reserve Challenge Certificate in both sexes at Crufts in 1983.

There are some other very dedicated Maltese breeders in Great Britain as well as those already mentioned. Mr. and Mrs. Lewin, who own the Challenge Certificate Winning Bitch from Crufts 1983, Champion Ellwin's Sweet Charity, breeder-owner-handled to complete her title at this event; Carol Hemsley, who owns the lovely Abbyat Oberon; Mrs. Blore, with the Movalians; and Mrs. Barratt with Bleathwood Silver Legend are among them.

Mrs. I. Salisbury and Mr. J. K. Salisbury are owners of the Bellebane Maltese at North Wales. Here resides, among others, the Top Winning Maltese of Ireland in 1982, Irish Champion Rahara Starbound, by Ellwin Royal Mint de Plata Pina ex Irish

Irish Ch. Pooltown The Aristocrat, Challenge Certificate and Green Star winner owned by Mrs. I. Salisbury, Bellebane Maltese, North Wales.

Champion Garryvoe Blue Star, who was bred by Miss R. Jacobs and is owned by Mr. Salisbury. To date this splendid dog has won fourteen Green Stars, Two Reserve Green Stars, Twelve Bests of Breed (including Best of Breed at the Maltese Club of Ireland Championship Show in 1981), first in the Toy Group at Bray Championship Show in 1982, and Reserve in Toy Group at the Combined Championship in 1983.

Then there is Irish Champion Pooltown The Aristocrat, by Champion Brantcliffe The Dictator ex Pooltown Satin Doll, bred by Mrs. E. Stephenson and owned by Mrs. I. Salisbury. The Aristocrat has thirteen Green Stars, one Reserve Green Star, two Challenge Certificates, and one Reserve Challenge Certificate, and five times has been Best of Breed, including at the Irish Kennel Club Championship Show in 1980.

The Aristocrat is the sire of Bellebane's Elegance of Pooltown, from Rahara Starsong of Bellebane, bred by Mrs. I. Salisbury and owned by Mrs. E. Stephenson. Wins to date for this one include one Challenge Certificate (Leicester Championship Show, 1982) and numerous additional honors at other championship shows.

The success of these dogs in both England and Ireland speaks well of their quality.

Canada's Top Dog for 1982 and Number Seven among all show dogs was a Maltese, American and Canadian Champion Revlo's Ringo Star. In addition to these victories, this exquisite bitch was shown twice in the United States the previous year, 1981, when she was twice awarded Best in Show, making her Number Fourteen Maltese in the States that year—truly a most beautiful and outstanding representative of her breed. She is owned by Gillian and Gordon Salls, who very understandably describe her as "the pride and joy" of their Petit Point Kennels, Reg., at Ardrossan, Alta. Ringo Star has been handled to her notable achievements by Elaine Mitchell and Tony Cumming.

Canada's Number Two Maltese for 1982 was Champion Chamonix Snow Cascade, while third in line during that year was Champion Snospark's Taste of Honey, who had been Number One in 1980. Honey, an American and Canadian Champion, is owned by Peter and Patti Scott and handled by Luke Ehricht.

Am. and Can. Ch. March'en Top Hat Dancer, one of the fine representatives of Marcia Hostetter's March'en Maltese at Des Moines, Iowa.

Ch. Snowgoose Valiant Lad (sitting) and Ch. Su-Le's Great Egret (lying). "Lad," top dog for 1982 in the United Kingdom, is owned by Snowgoose Kennels in England. "Egret" is owned by Andreas Hynes of Australia.

Australian fanciers are great dog lovers, and the activity there among them seems to increase with every passing year. The Maltese is highly appreciated, and some very fine ones are being raised by Australian breeders, as I have learned from friends who are among the many Americans visiting dog shows in that country as judges.

Just as we are writing this book, a very lovely little dog from one of our leading American kennels is becoming established in Sydney, having been imported by Mrs. Andrea Hynes. He is American and Canadian Champion Su-Le's Great Egret, formerly owned by Barbara Bergquist of the famed Su-Le Maltese. Since Su-Le is noted not only for *winners* but for dogs which *reproduce quality*, Egret should prove a valuable addition to the Maltese Fancy in Australia, and be very popular with breeders as a stud dog.

Sydney is also the home of an English lady who came originally to Australia from Yorkshire, Mrs. Nell Henman, who is meeting with enormous success as a breeder-exhibitor. Her first Maltese, a dog named Hollyhock Snowglen was purchased from

Mrs. C. Cross. He did a bit of winning for her and at the same time Mrs. Henman's enthusiasm for the breed grew to the point where she knew that she wanted more of these dogs; to raise them, and to have an Australian champion. She went about it the right way with the purchase of three excellent bitches from Ted Tancred's kennel. The first of these was Cozyvista Estner, followed very shortly by Cozyvista I Had A Dream and Cozyvista Swan Song. Thus Mrs. Henman was provided with three truly lovely bitches on which to base a breeding program. Soon all had become champions, and Mrs. Henman's kennel name, Maltoi, for her future breeding program had been selected.

In August 1979 the first Maltoi litter was born, from Champion Cozyvista Estner sired by Champion Cozyvista Kolara. Included among the three puppies was one which became Champion Maltoi Classic Aaron, now a Best in Show winner.

Ch. Cozyvista I Had A Dream was bred to a New Zealand importation, Champion Miracle Snowflake, subsequently producing Champion Maltoi Kimberley Royale, who gained her title at fourteen months and has now become Number 1 Maltese Bitch in New South Wales. Her successes have included Best of Breed at the 1982 Sydney Royal Easter Show, followed later in the year by victories at Brisbane's National and at the R.A.S. Kennel Control's Spring Championship. Climax for the year for this beautiful bitch was winning Best in Show at the New South Wales Maltese Specialty.

Champion Cozyvista Swan Song was scheduled for breeding to the new import, Mrs. Hynes' American and Canadian Champion Su-Le's Great Egret. An event anticipated with keen excitement! We hope that the puppies from this mating have turned out extraordinarily well, as indeed should be the case when one considers the splendid quality of their background!

At the recent Spring Dog Show of the Royal Agricultural Society Kennel Control, at Sydney, Australia, in October 1983, 41 Maltese were entered. Best of Breed here was New Zealand Champion Patrician Pontefract, an import from New Zealand, sired by New Zealand Champion Vicbrita Park Royal, who had been brought to New Zealand from England, representing the famed Vicbrita blood-lines, out of New Zealand Champion Iluan Primavera. Mrs. P. Alton of Casula, New South Wales, owns this splendid dog who was born in May 1978. Reserve Best of Breed was Champion Yandjana Elwin, owned by the Misses I.E. and M.R. Sutton, Belmore, New South Wales. This bitch, born in October 1980, is a daughter of English and Australian Champion Ellwin Royal Jubilation, imported from the United Kingdom, ex Silvertail Sno Juliet. The Suttons also showed Champion Yandjana Elwin Tobias, a litter brother to Kristen, and their sire, English and Australian Champion Ellwin Royal Jubilation, who is a son of English Champion Francoombe Fancy Star Turn ex Ellwin Albina Mia, whelped April 1977, along with some puppies.

Mrs. Alton, in addition to her Best of Breed dog, had a winning puppy bitch in Pascale Chantilly Lace, by Jamabeco Tristian ex Jamabeco Sweet Lacey.

Champion Jocasta Tiger Lily won Open Bitch and Reserve for the Certificate for Mrs. E.R. Lunardi, Greystanes, New South Wales. This bitch is by Australian Champion Shadyway Little Tiger ex Australian Champion Whiteair Tamara Danca, and was born in 1979. Reserve among the dogs was the Australian bred Champion Velette Dubois, born April 1980, by Champion Manalee Mischa ex Champion Velette La Fleur, owned by Mrs. S.J. Stocks, Kellyville, New South Wales.

Australian Champion Patrician Paris Model completed title just as we are writing, owned by Mrs. A. Pervushin, Hazelbrook, New South Wales. This New Zealand importation is by New Zealand Champion Patrician Peeping Tom ex Patrician Paris Mist.

Ckisiane Maltese, owned by Miss P.A. Neylan, at Hamilton, Coriedaxston Kennels owned by Mrs. J.E. Musker, Baulkham Hills, Cottontails Kennels, Mrs. M.J. James; Dulcibella, Mrs. J. Johns; Jascoal, Mrs. S.L. Coco; Kalmist, Mrs. J. Hall; Maledka, Mrs. W.A. Kaveney; Plumosa, Mrs. P.J. Rosen; Santanton Kennels, Mrs. R. Attard; Sheridav, Mrs. G.M. Back; Sindale Kennels, Mrs. D.R. Sinclair; Snopampas, Mrs. B. Whitelaw; Spitfire, Miss K.A. Spiteri; Tacoma, Mrs. K.F. Schuppe; Tammadav Kennels, Mrs. M. Napier; Tammwham Kennels, Mrs. M.A. Robbins; Toyjoy, Misses J. and A. Holdstock; Wilcott Kennels, Mrs. D.M. Mottershead; Winajo, Mrs. N. McKelvey; are all among the Maltese Kennels in the New South Wales area where quality Maltese are raised.

Ch. To The Victor of Eng, sire of 65 U.S.A. champions, 9 Canadian champions, and others in other countries, here is winning his fifth "major" to become a champion at age 1 year under the famed breeder judge Aennchen Antonelli, of Aennchen's Maltese, owner-handled by Barbara Bergquist at Western Reserve Kennel Club, December 1970.

Chapter III
Maltese in the
United States

Although the breed was known and owned here for at least two decades prior to the 1950's, it could quite truthfully be stated that the United States "discovered" the Maltese and that its rise to fame and popularity in American show rings came about during the decade of the 1950's. It was then that they began consistently hitting the "big time" winning and that fanciers and judges in the United States really started taking these charming little white dogs to their hearts.

Several events contributed to this happening. Possibly the foremost event was the appearance, in big city show rings (New York, Boston, and Chicago among others), of Dr. Vincenzo Calvaresi with his fantastic Maltese team. Four perfectly matched little beauties who worked together almost as a single dog, trained and handled always by Dr. Calvaresi himself. Dr. and Mrs. Calvaresi had been Maltese breeders since the 1930's, and along with Miss Hannah Mee Horner, another very astute breeder, exhibitor, and devotee of the breed, had been loyal in their support of it and of presenting fine Maltese dogs at leading events in the eastern United States. Dr. Calvaresi's dogs came, in many cases, from the Hale Farm Kennels and from abroad, from which foundation stock he and his wife eventually produced many a Best in Show winner. They were located in Massachusetts. Hannah Mee Horner, on the other hand, was from the Pennsylvania area and had one of the breed's early Toy Group winners in her very handsome Champion Skytop White Flash. It could be said that Miss Horner was one of the first to place particular emphasis on quality of coat, and I have heard her on many occasions explaining the *true* coat, single and free of undercoat, curl, or waviness, to newer students of the breed.

One of Dr. Vincenzo
Calvaresi's earliest
Maltese back in 1948.

Dr. Vincenzo Calvaresi, a pioneer Maltese breeder, with the team he made world-famous is here winning Best Team in Show at Chicago-International with four of his outstanding dogs in April 1956. These little Maltese created a sensation wherever they appeared, and had many similar honors to their credit at Westminster and other major shows. Mrs. C. Groverman Ellis, President of the Club, is presenting the award. John P. Wagner is the judge.

As a teen-ager, with special permission from her school to be absent in order to show her little dog at Westminster, Anna Marie Stimmler won Best of Breed in 1964 with Ch. Co Ca He's Aennchen's Toy Dancer, which then went on to Best Toy for a spectacular victory.

The Calvaresis, right from the beginning, consistently exhibited large entries in their area. Their early stock included Cupid of Villa Malta (Snow Flurry of Hale Farm ex Circe of Hale Farm), who was born in 1935 and was bred by Miss Eleanor C. Bancroft; Manon of Villa Malta (Cupid of Hale Farm ex Vira of Villa Malta), a homebred born in 1941; and Mimi (Sonny Boy of Hale Farm ex Hale Farms Hermanita), also homebred, born in 1942. There was also Musette of Villa Malta and a bitch named Linda, along with two dogs, Citane of Villa Malta and Lindoro of Villa Malta, the latter three all by Cupid of Hale Farm. Thus it would seem that Cupid deserves credit as the dominant stud dog behind the Villa Malta strain. Later came importations, Champion Electa Pampi and Champion Electa Brio of Villa Malta, also still to be found in Villa Malta pedigrees.

Miss Horner, on a smaller scale, was breeding throughout this period, too, mostly line-breeding from her own stock. The aforementioned Flash was probably her best known winner and was a truly lovely dog. Skytop Happyone and Skytop Darlene were two of her good bitches, both by Skytop Peterkin. And in the late 1940's she brought out the quality bitch, Champion Skytop Felicity.

Mrs. Bertha Watkins was another early Pennsylvania fancier, having imported, from England's famed Invicta Kennels, the successful Champion Invicta Dina of Questover. She also had foundation stock from Villa Malta, a dog and a bitch sired by Champion Nino of Villa Malta.

The original Villa Malta team consisted of Champion Tristan of Villa Malta, C.D.X., Champion Taro of Villa Malta, Champion Rico of Vilia Malta, and Champion Renee of Villa Malta. The Calvaresis also were consistent winners in brace competition, but this paled somewhat as compared to the excitement created by the *four* sparkling little dogs who made up the always precise and perfect team. These four dogs certainly did more than any single factor to make people wish to own a Maltese, and the honors they brought home, in both Group Team and Best in Show Team competition, were both numerous and impressive. There were replacements occasionally among the team dogs as time progressed, but all performed in the expected manner, adding up to a spectacle to truly thrill ringsiders and bring down the house!

This team of dogs was not alone as an event making the 1950's of particular importance to the Maltese world! It was during the

Ch. Talia of Villa Malta seems to be smiling as she wins the Toy Group for Dr. and Mrs. Vincenzo Calvaresi at Woodstock on the New England Circuit in 1963. Marge Rozik handled her.

This picture carrying much nostalgia is of Dr. Calvaresi owner-handling one of his early Best in Show winning bitches, Ch. Talia of Villa Malta. Talia took Best Toy at Philadelphia Kennel Club Dog Show in 1958 under another famed Maltese breeder, Miss Hannah Mee Horner, a pioneer fancier of these tiny white dogs, owner of the Skytop Kennels, and a popular Toy judge.

The great Ch. Aennchen's Poona Dancer, Larry Ward's and Frank Oberstar's exciting bitch, handled by her owner to Best in Show at the Progressive Dog Club in 1966.

What a host of admirers Best in Show winner Ch. Pendleton's Jewel garnered during her career with her owner-handler Mrs. Dorothy White from Ohio! Here she is gaining one of a great many Toy Group victories at the huge Trenton Kennel Club event in 1970 where the judge was Joe Faigel.

A Christmas present from Eng. Ch. Gosmore Vicbrita Tristan, England's outstanding sire by Eng. Ch. Vicbrita Tobias ex Vicbrita Serpolette. Mrs. A. Dallison, owner, Gosmore Maltese, Gerrards Cross, Bucks.

The exquisite Eng. Ch. Gosmore Mayhems Jannette, by Vicbrita Vitesse ex Malcolm's Miracle of Barbella, one of the many outstanding Maltese at Gosmore Kennels, Mrs. A. Dallison, Gerrards Cross, Bucks, England.

mid-fifties that Anne and Stewart Pendleton started winning a whole series of Toy Groups and Best in Show with a marvelous bitch, Champion Brittigan's Dark Eyes (Champion Quenell Buttons and Beaux ex Champion Tammie of Tamalene) under the handling of Wynn Suck. These Ohio fanciers showed their lovely bitch consistently and fearlessly and she aroused tremendous admiration for her breed.

Then it was in the 1950's that a charming, vibrant, and talented lady, Mrs. J. P. (Aennchen) Antonelli, joined the ranks of Maltese fanciers, leading to a whole series of Aennchen-bred winners as the years progressed. In the mid-fifties, Aennchen and her husband, Tony, were winning with Champion Aennchen's Raja Yoga, who gained titular honors in both the United States and Bermuda. Raja Yoga sired at least a dozen champions, including the great Champion Aennchen's Shikar Dancer who became one of the breed's most dominant sires as well as show dogs under the ownership of Joanne Hesse (Joanne-Chen Maltese). He numbered among his progeny such record-breakers as Champion Aennchen's Sari Dancer, Champion Co-Ca-He's Aennchen's Toy Dancer, Champion Joanne-Chen's Sweet Shi Dancer, Champion Joanne-Chen's Shicka Dancer, and Champion Joanne-Chen's Shikar Dancer.

Champion Aennchen's Joanne-Chen's Shikar Dancer was a son of American and Bermudian Champion Aennchen's Raja Yoga, his dam having been Champion Aennchen's Puja Dancer. He became an American champion when only eight months old.

Aennchen's success as a breeder of outstanding Maltese was fantastic. Among those to her credit have been Champion Aennchen's Tala Dancer (Champion Aennchen's Raja Yoga ex Aennchen's Jon Vir Royal Gopi), Champion Aennchen's Poona Dancer (Champion Aennchen's Siva Dancer ex Aennchen Santal Dancer), Champion Aennchen's Sari Dancer (Champion Aennchen's Shikar Dancer ex Aennchen's Raga Dancer), Champion Aennchen's Sitar Dancer (Aennchen's Manushya Dancer ex Champion Aennchen's Smart Dancer), Champion Aennchen's Pipal Dancer (Champion Aennchen's Siva Dancer ex Aennchen's G.G. Dancer), Champion Aennchen's Shakti Dancer (same parents as above), Champion Aennchen's Savar Dancer (Siva Dancer ex Sitar Dancer), and Champion Aennchen's Tasia Dancer (Siva Dancer ex Champion Aennchen's Taja Dancer), the latter co-owned with Nicholas Cutillo, who has carried on with Aennchen breeding following this lady's death.

Aennchen Antonelli lost her fight with cancer during the 1970's, and Maltese lost one of its greatest, most knowledgeable breeders. Aennchen's contributions to Maltese are countless, as one realizes in noting the number of winning pedigrees tracing back to her dogs. Added to these is the fact that she was always eager to encourage and to be helpful to others—a great lady whom our entire Fancy misses sincerely.

Joanne Hesse, famous in her own right as the lady behind Joanne-Chen Maltese, founded her own kennels on Aennchen's strain, acquiring her early winners and breeding stock there. She, too has possessed fantastic talents as a breeder, which one has but to glance at the number of outstanding Joanne-Chen dogs in the show ring and behind some of the breed's leading winners to confirm. Champion Aennchen's Shikar Dancer was acquired by Mrs. Hesse as a puppy from the Antonellis. Among the early homebreds on Mrs. Hesse's credit list are Champion Joanne-Chen's Shikar Dancer, a Best in Show dog for Harmo Kennels under Bill Trainor's handling; Champion Joanne-Chen's Sweet Shi Dancer; Champion Joanne-Chen's Shika Dancer; Champion Joanne-Chen's Maya Dancer, noted Best in Show winner owned by Mamie R. Gregory; and Champion Joanne-Chen's Square Dancer; all of these dogs, with their descendants, hold prominent positions in the record of Maltese progress in the United States!

Returning again to the mid-fifties, Elvera Cox with her Fairy Fay dogs were becoming well known, including Champion Fairy Fay Figaro. Rose Sloan was starting out Champion Caprice of Kismet, a homebred sired by Champion Aennchen's Raja Yoga. And film star Gary Cooper had discovered Maltese, with his Champion Tina of Yelwa being campaigned by Mitch Wooten.

Throughout this time, Villa Malta had been extremely active, and as we entered the 1960's, they were pointing with pride to their Best in Show dogs, Champion Musi of Villa Malta, Champion Lacy of Villa Malta, and Champion Talia of Villa Malta—all an enormous credit to the breed!

In California, Miriam Thompson was breeding some fine Maltese under the Sun Canyon banner. Some of these came East, where I had the pleasure of judging them and thought them dogs of type and quality.

Can. and Am. Ch. Villa Malta's Jessigo Bear "just resting" between ring appearances. Bred by Marge Rozik, Villa Malta Kennels, this lovely dog belongs to Joy and Ed Woodard, Gresham, Arizona.

Ch. Bar None Buckineer, an outstanding winner from Bar None Kennels, Michele Perlmutter, Ghent, New York.

Highest Scoring Dog in Trial, Nassau, Bahamas, March 1983. Ch. Ginger Jake U.D., Can. C.D.X. and Baha. C.D., looks proud and happy as he again distinguishes himself for his owner, Faith Maciejewski, West Allis, Wisconsin.

Following the big successes of their Champion Brittigan's Dark Eyes in the mid-1950's, Anne and Stewart Pendleton brought out a younger brother from a repeat of the same breeding. This was Champion Brittigan's Sweet William, who, although he did not attain quite the heights Dark Eyes had reached, made a good showing. Then there were some interesting homebreds for this couple, including Champion Pendleton's Picadore, from Champion Salley's Wee Magic of Melitaie ex the famous Champion Brittigan's Dark Eyes; Pendleton's Cotton Candy, from Champion Salley's Wee Magic of Melitaie ex Wrenn's Snowball; and Champion Pendleton's Try Baby from a daughter of Sweet William ex Pendleton's Spring Day among them. They also owned several Maltese which had been bred by Salley A. Horton: Champion Salley's Lady Leah of Melitaie and Salley's Lady Lisa of Melitaie, from two separate litters, both by Jon Vir's Gay Adventurer ex Champion Little Duchess of Jon Vir. The famous bitch which started Dorothy White off on an exciting winning whirl, leading to her continued enthusiasm for the Fancy as a Maltese owner and as a professional handler, bore the Pendleton kennel prefix although not bred by them, Champion Pendleton's Jewel. Bred by Venus Ann Davison, this fantastic little bitch was a daughter of Davison's Toby Image of Toto ex Venus Ann's Sparkle. She and Dottie White made an impressive pair as they swept the boards at show after show—an exquisite Maltese always faultlessly presented. They made their presence felt in keenest competition around the United States.

It was in the mid-1960's that Frank Oberstar, known to present-day fanciers as a well-qualified and popular multi-breed judge, was making history as an owner-handler with a superb Maltese, Champion Aennchen's Poona Dancer (Champion Aennchen's Siva Dancer ex Aennchen's Santal Dancer), whelped September 1963, bred by Mr. and Mrs. J. P. Antonelli, and co-owned by Frank Oberstar and Larry G. Ward. Poona broke all sorts of records for the day, becoming one of history's greats.

The Oberstar-Ward kennel housed some other fine Maltese as well, including Champion Starward's Gulliver (Champion J. G. Mr. Playboy ex Glanneln's Hello Dolly), born September 1967 and bred by H. M. Young; and Ch. Aennchen's Pipal Dancer, bred by the Antonellis, by Champion Aennchen's Siva Dancer ex Aennchen's G. G. Dancer.

Ch. Brittigan's Sweet William, Maltese dog, winning Best in Show at Rubber City Kennel Club, Akron, Ohio, June 1961. Mr. and Mrs. Stewart Pendleton, owners; Wynn Suck, handler. The judge was Maxwell Riddle.

Gene Stimmler handling his sister's Ch. Aennchen's Sari Dancer to win a Toy Group from Anna K. Nicholas in 1965. Sari Dancer was later owned by Michael Wolf in his Mike-Mark Kennels show and breeding program.

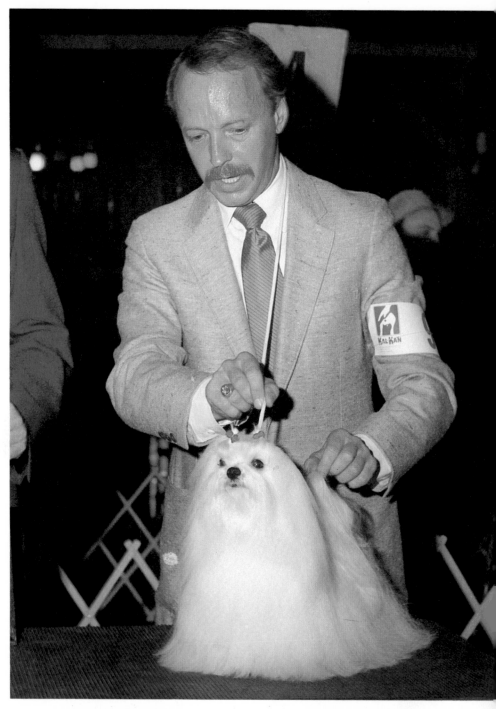

The noted multiple Group winning Ch. Aennchen's Ruari Dancer was bred by Nicholas Cutillo, is owned by Barry Giske, and handled here by Bud Dickey.

Ch. Carlinda's Latest Sensation, a homebred belonging to Martha and Linda DiGiovanni, handled by Terence Childs. Photo courtesy of Mr. Childs.

Ch. Nicholas of Al-Mar, bred by Marjorie Lewis, owned by Norma Kantelis, going Best in Show (in the rain) at the Ladies Dog Club in 1979.

Ch. Joanne-Chen's Shikar Dancer brought many honors to Harmo Kennels in the 1960s. Here, with handler William Trainor, she is going Best in Show on one of these occasions.

Gwen Holbrook for quite awhile was a successful Maltese exhibitor whose best known winners of this period were the lovely Champion Aennchen's Imp of Gwenbrook, born in 1966, and Mike Mar's Gwenbrook, born in 1970.

Michael Wolf, of Mike Mar Kennels, is one of our most famous breeder-owner-handlers of many breeds of dogs today, including Pekingese, Pomeranians, Chow Chows, Boston Terriers, Italian Greyhounds, and numerous others. In the 1960's, he appeared at dog shows with Maltese, and Mike Mar has contributed much to the progress of this breed, as Michael has never completely lost his interest in it and is a breeder of well-above-average talents. Among his early winners, and the foundation stock on which Mike Mar Maltese are based, were a bitch, Joanne-Chen's Merry Dancer, who, bred to Champion Joanne-Chen's Hadji Dancer, produced well and included among the progeny was Champion Mike Mar's Maji Puff (born 1966) who went to Rena Martin for her breeding program. Champion Mike Mar's Devil Dancer and Champion Mike Mar's Poetry in Motion were littermates, by Champion Co Ca He's Aennchen's Raja Dancer ex Debbies White Penny, born in 1966 and bred by Nan Bennett Sorcordies. In 1968-69, Mr. Wolf added to his kennel the spectacular winning Best in Show bitch, Champion Aennchen's Sari Dancer, one of the loveliest Maltese I have known, who was purchased from the Stimmlers. Throughout the years since then, Mike Mar Maltese have been in the limelight in the United States and in Canada, and the champions bred by Michael Wolf must add up to an impressive total.

Mrs. Robert M. Stuber was showing Maltese back in the 1960's and is a lady who has contributed much to this breed. Champion Beland Little Smarty (by Champion Fidino of Villa Malta ex Champion Beland Miss Cuddles), born in 1964 and bred by Mrs. F. M. Peacock, belonged to her. Champion Andrena of Primrose Place (Champion Robby of Primrose Place ex Champion Vicbrite Rozeta), born in 1963, was a homebred of hers as was Primrose Betty Boo (Champion Freemont of Valletta ex Primrose Raggedy Ann), born in 1969. Primrose Little Toot of Al-Mar, bred by Marjorie Lewis, by Champion Tiny Scooter of Al-Mar ex Champion Tiny Tila Lee of Al-Mar, born in 1966, was one she owned; and in the late 1960's she added to her Maltese family Joanne-Chen's Magi Dancer, by Champion

Michele Perlmutter owner-handling her lovely bitch, Bar None The One and Only to Winners Bitch at the 1983 American Maltese Association National Specialty in 1983. Mrs. Keke Blumberg judging.

Opposite: This delightful youngster is Ch. Paper Doll of Al-Mar, bred by Marjorie Lewis, owner-handled by Dee Shepherd, Bryantville, Mass.

This Best in Show winning Maltese is Ch. Mil-Ottie's Molly B. handled by Bennie Dennard, owned by Dorothy Hochrein and received a top award from Louis Murr at Greater Miami Dog Club in June 1971.

Alekai Kennels, owned by Mrs. Henry J. Kaiser, did much winning in the early 1960s with Ch. Aennchen's Smart Dancer handled by Wendell J. Sammet. Judge pictured is Alva Rosenberg, at the Jacksonville Dog Fanciers, January 1962.

Joanne-Chen's Teddy Bear ex Champion Joanne-Chen's Aga Lynn Dancer, born November 1968 and bred by Joanne Hesse.

Marjorie Lewis, Al-Mar Kennels, has been a steady breeder of Maltese over a very long period of time and is as well a professional handler. Dr. Kenneth Knopf and his daughter, Samantha, were owners of such important winners as Champion Anna Marie's White Panther and Champion Aennchen's Paris Dancer.

Nancy H. Shapland, of White Heath, Illinois, has been a lady prominent in the Maltese limelight with some truly glorious bitches. Who ever could forget The Flying Nun, a little bitch that literally "swept the boards" in keenest competition throughout the United States under Peggy Hogg's expert handling? And after her retirement, she was followed by Champion Malone's Snowy Roxanne, another one who pleased the judges, again handled by Peggy Hogg.

Doreen Wilkinson is a breeder always seen with some good ones. Many of her Gayla dogs carry the combined Gayla-Joanne-Chen kennel prefix, indicating a strong influx of the Joanne-Chen bloodlines.

Barbara Dempsey Alderman, noted professional handler who divides her time between Florida and Pennsylvania, has long been a good friend to the Maltese. Her charges have included a steady procession of outstanding winners, and watching her presentation of them is always a delight to the eye.

There are many, many others throughout the United States about whom we would love to tell you if space permitted. The Maltese is, indeed, a well-owned breed, belonging to people who truly appreciate the exquisite dogs with which they are associated.

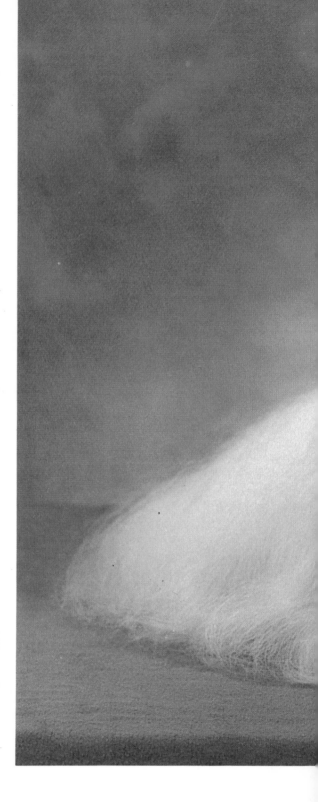

This is "Missy", Ch.
So Big's Desert
Delight, dam of Ch.
Rebecca's Desert
Valentino, owned by
Mrs. Freda Tinsley,
Rebecca's Maltese,
Scottsdale, Arizona.

Best Brace in Toy Group at Westminster 1969, judged by Anna Katherine Nicholas, was won by Ch. Martin's Jingles Puff (a Best in Show winner) and Ch. Martin's Bangles Puff, handled by Daryl Martin for her mother, Rena Martin. The Martins, in addition to being successful professional handlers, are long-time breeders of highest quality Maltese.

Chapter IV
Maltese Kennels in the
United States

There is no better way to describe the progress of a breed than by telling you of the individual breeders and kennels who have contributed along the way and of those who are currently active. We have selected a cross section of the latter with which to supplement our chapter of breed history in the United States, presenting some of the current leading winners and summarizing the backgrounds from which they have been produced.

A kennel name is important to a breeder, and one should be selected and used from the time of your first homebred litter onward. Kennel names are chosen in many different ways. Some folks select the street on which they live with which to identify their dogs. Others will use their name (either first or last) such as Aennchen's or Martin's. Some will take a child's name (Rebecca's) when that youngster is especially enthused over and involved with the dogs. Then there are kennel names "coined" from a combined part of the owners' own names or those of their children. Mike Mar was so named by Michael Wolf, combining MIKE from his own name with MARgaret from his mother's name, as she always was interested in and involved with Michael's earliest dogs which included Maltese. Or the name of an important early dog owned by you and influential to your kennel can be chosen, either the proper name or call name. Whatever strikes your fancy and is appropriate makes a good choice and will identify the Maltese which you yourself have bred throughout future generations.

Kennel names can be registered with the American Kennel Club, which gives you the exclusive right to that name in registering dogs, and no other breeder or owner can use it without your consent during the period of registration. You can

Ch. Aennchen Ethanbert Snow Dance, by Ch. Aennchen's Shiko Dancer ex Ch. Ethanbert Miss Lacey Love, is co-owned by Nicholas Cutillo, Ethel Eppich and Elizabeth Rumohr and now retired, after a highly successful whirlwind career in the show ring, living at Ethanbert Kennels in Franklin, West Virginia. Handled by Mr. Cutillo.

receive detailed information regarding this by contacting the American Kennel Club, 51 Madison Avenue, New York, N.Y. 10010. There are certain requirements regarding the type of name eligible for registration, and a fee is to be paid if one chooses this course.

To be of greatest value, kennel names should be applied only to dogs bred by that kennel, as then it immediately identifies the dog and its background. As breeding programs continue, they each establish a type of their own most times. As Maltese breeder Peggy Lloyd has pointed out, and given us permission to quote:

> In future years when the involved dogs are gone and no longer available for current breeders to see, then newcomers will be able to view photos of dogs with a particular kennel name and immediately note the fact that ZZZ Kennels produced short-backed little dogs with babydoll faces, while XXX Kennel dogs were more up on the leg and had straighter, silkier coats. If the dog has several kennel names, which have been added by other owners to the original, are future breeders to assume that it looks like a ZZZ dog or like an XXX dog? Of course, every dog has more than one bloodline in its background. However, each breeder has his or her "type" of Maltese in his mind's eye, and most of that person's dogs will lean toward that type.

To correctly fulfill its purpose, a kennel name should be used in registering each of your homebreds and on them exclusively, so that future breeders looking at a pedigree can tell exactly what to expect in characteristics of the dog it has produced.

On the following pages we pay tribute to some of our long-time breeders and some of the newer ones. On the shoulders of the latter squarely rests the task of carrying on and preserving what has been accomplished and the responsibility for the future well-being of the Maltese breed.

Aennchen (Nicholas Cutillo)

In our previous chapter dealing with earlier Maltese in the United States, we have written a good deal about Aennchen Antonelli, her impact as a breeder of outstanding Maltese and the influence of these dogs on future generations of Maltese right up until the present time. I am sure that every dedicated breeder must wish that there would be someone interested enough and well liked and respected by that breeder who could "carry on" a breeding program into which years of love, thought, study, and devotion had been poured, keeping the kennel name and the basic breeding principles alive as that person would have done personally. It seems appropriate that a lady who gave as much of herself to furthering the interests of others as Aennchen did through her dogs should have had such a friend. And that, since her death in the early 1970's that friend—Nicholas Cutillo, whose own kennel and breeding program were based upon the Aennchen line, in keeping with Aennchen Antonelli's wish—is continuing to use the Aennchen prefix.

Ch. Aennchen's Stela Dancer, by Ch. Aennchen's Soomi Dancer ex Aennchen's Kara Dancer, finished in 5 shows, undefeated, with several Group placements. Owned by Nicholas Cutillo, New York City, who is handling her. Edna Ackerman, judge.

Ch. Oak Ridge Country 'N Lace as a 6-month-old puppy shows you how a promising youngster should look at this age. By Ch. Infante Mystic Caper (his last litter) ex Oak Ridge Sand Pebble. Carol A. Neth owner-handler.

BEST OF
WINNERS
CARROLL
KENNEL CLUB
82
ASHBEY II

The famed Ch. Aennchen's Poona Dancer seems to be smiling as she gains the Best in Show award for owners Frank Oberstar and L.G. Ward (Mr. Oberstar handling) at Rock Creek Kennel Club in 1967. A superb Maltese in every way. Robert Waters, judge.

Nicholas Cutillo, living then at Lodi, New Jersey, became acquainted with Maltese in 1961 through his high school art instructor, Tony Antonelli, who was Aennchen's husband. Tony was in the habit of bringing press clippings reviewing the successes of such famed winners as Champion Aennchen's Poona Dancer and Champion Co Ca He's Aennchen's Toy Dancer to class to share with his pupils. So great was young Nick's interest that he was invited to visit the Antonellis at home, to meet Aennchen and to see her beautiful dogs.

After graduation from high school, Mr. Cutillo immediately set about acquiring his first Maltese. It had been suggested that he contact Aga Lynn Kennels, from where he took home with him an eight-month-old bitch, Aennchen's Yuki of Aga Lynn, daughter of Champion Aennchen's Timhi Dancer and Joanne-Chen's Fan Dancer. Yuki turned out to be somewhat of a disappointment, which can happen with puppies, as she never won a point. As a reward for his continued interest and dedication, the Antonellis presented him with Champion Aennchen's Tasia Dancer, Poona Dancer's half-sister, both by Champion Aennchen's Siva Dancer, her dam another Best in Show winner, Champion Aennchen's Taja Dancer. Tasia succeeded handsomely where Yuki had not, completing her championship at the American Maltese Association Specialty in 1972, held in conjunction with the Chicago International, where she not only went to Best of Winners but also won Best of Opposite Sex over Specials. Later she went on to a good Specials career which included Group placements.

Probably the greatest learning experience that any young Maltese fancier possibly could have came to Nick Cutillo when he was showing Yuki and Tasie, as Aennchen was herself campaigning Champion Aennchen's Savar Dancer at the time, and she and Nick drove together to many dog shows—talking, we are sure, about Maltese every mile of the way on each trip—and at the show. Additionally, Nick would help Aennchen with the grooming as she demonstrated for him how it should be done to best advantage.

The next Maltese to join those at Mr. Cutillo's was Champion Aennchen's Pompi Dancer (Champion Aennchen's Taran Dancer ex Aennchen's Sharika Dancer) who produced for him three litters of a single puppy each, all of whom became champions. Champion Pompi, born in 1971, is still well and happy as we write in 1983.

It was at about this period that Aennchen's physical condition took a turn for the worse, and her friends all rallied around to help. The last dog her health permitted her to personally show was Champion Aennchen's Savar Dancer, who was used sparingly at stud. The last litter bred by Aennchen and Tony Antonelli was by this dog from Aennchen's Sharika Dancer, born during July 1972. All three became champions. One of these, which the Antonellis had held back from selling, was given to Nick Cutillo as a birthday gift, becoming Champion Aennchen's Soomi Dancer, weighing in at three and three-quarter pounds. Making his ring debut, he promptly took Winners, Best of Winners, and

Ch. Martin's Annabel-Cid, by Ch. Martin's Michael-Cid ex Chris's Sugar, winning under judge Robert Wills, handled by Barbara Alderman for Marjorie Martin, Columbus, Ohio.

Ch. Aennchen's Sari Dancer, at that time owned by Anna Marie Stimmler, winning Best in Show at Penn Treaty in 1965. Her owner's brother, Gene Stimmler, is handling this lovely Maltese here.

then Best of Breed, setting the pace for a highly successful show career. Shown as a Special only nineteen times, he won the breed on all but one of these occasions, became a Group winner, and annexed some half dozen Group placements. Soomi has an American Maltese Association Award as the sire of five champions, each of which gained admirable distinction. The champions who earned the award for him were Champion Yogi Nimble Vic, (Group winner), Aennchen's Stela Dancer (finished undefeated and with Group placements), Aennchen's Cari Krsna Dancer, Ethanbert's Miss Lacy Love, and Rolynda D'Aennchen.

Just at the time when Aennchen's health was failing most severely, the Antonellis saw and fell in love with a two-pound nine-ounce bitch, so beautiful that they considered her, to quote Mr. Cutillo, "sheer perfection." She had been bred by Mrs.

Jerline Brooker, was a daughter of Champion Joanne-Chen's Mini Man Dancer ex BenJerbe's Juliette DiNeve, and grew up to become Champion Jerline's Libra Dancer. As Aennchen was too ill to campaign this lovely bitch herself, she was given to Mr. Cutillo to show, who finished her in no time flat with wins which included two five-point majors.

Aennchen's Kara Dancer belonged to famed Italian journalist, Chiara Pisani, who bred her to Savar. They produced Champion Aennchen's Shiko Dancer, who was eventually given to Mr. Cutillo. This dog was shown only sparingly, but he made his principal claim to fame as a stud dog, gaining an Award from the Maltese Dog Association as the sire of eight champions: Aennchen's Cari Apollo Dancer and Aennchen's Cari Jyoti Dancer (littermates), Aennchen's Indra Dancer, Le Sheik Dancer Du Barrie, Aennchen's Jnani Dancer, Aennchen's Ananda Dancer, and Aennchen's Soada Dancer. Shiko died in August 1982, a true loss to the breed.

To his previously entirely Aennchen line-breeding program, following Mrs. Antonelli's death, when breeding had ceased in the original Aennchen kennel, Mr. Cutillo decided that he needed some new bitches to use with his own stock. Thus he added one descended from the Good Time line of a similar background to that behind Aennchen's first dogs, based, as hers had been, on Jon Vir and Villa Malta. This bitch produced Champion Aennchen's Indra Dancer and Aennchen's Siimi Dancer, littermates. Siimi is co-owned with Mrs. Betty M. Charpie and has made a good name for herself, having given her owners the lovely Champion Aennchen's Ruari Dancer, now owned by Barry Giske for whom he is now a Group winner.

Champion Aennchen's Ashur Dancer also was sired by Siimi, completed an early title (at eleven months), and, as we write, is preparing for a Specials career. Aennchen's Kamilah Dancer and Aennchen's Buddhi Yoga Dancer are two Siimi daughters who should be sporting the "champion" title by the time you are reading this. Co-owned by Miss Stacey Brooks of Phoenix, Arizona, Ashur Dancer is being shown in that area of the country.

Champion Aennchen's Arjuna Dancer is one of the newer champions at Mr. Cutillo's, and Aennchen's Soomi Sun Dancer, one of very few Soomi Dancer sons, is already pointed although still a puppy.

Ch. Villa Malta's Timmy, owned by Doris Wexler and bred by Marge Rozik, Villa Malta Kennels, finishing his title under the author.

Youthful Anna Marie Stimmler takes Best in Show with her exciting sensation of the mid-1960s, Ch. Co Ca He's Aennchen's Toy Dancer. The judge is Mrs. Ramona Van Court Jones.

The Aennchen Maltese live in happy home surroundings, as was the case at Aennchen's own establishment. Show dogs and youngsters being prepared for the ring live in New York City with Nick Cutillo himself (he is a very famous fashion designer with a busy schedule to maintain), while the older ones and the retirees live with his parents in New Jersey. Some are co-owned with other fanciers, as for instance those already mentioned above. In addition, Mr. Cutillo works closely with the Maltese with Mrs. Betty Charpie, Char Mar Maltese at Cleveland, Ohio, whose dogs are also basically Aennchen breeding.

Long a hard-working member of the American Maltese Association, Nick Cutillo now serves as its President and is also its Delegate to the American Kennel Club. He also is a former President of the Metropolitan Area Maltese Association and belongs to several other Maltese Specialty Clubs in various sections of the United States. Mr. Cutillo is truly a very dedicated fancier.

Bar None

Bar None Maltese, at Ghent, New York, are owned by Michele Perlmutter, a young lady who has had tremendous success both as a breeder and as an exhibitor. It all started as the result of her family having bought a Miniature Pinscher some years back, while they were living in Texas. Michele and her sister both love dogs so much and had just lost the family dog which they had owned since Michele was age three. This Min Pin was the girls' first purebred and had been purchased, with papers, for $35.00

The girls started taking the Min Pin to obedience classes, and the handler in charge suggested that they try him out in conformation competition. They did a few times in Texas before moving east and won a few blue ribbons.

Ch. Bar None Big Man On Campus finished for title under judge Richard Hammond, handled by Dee Shepherd for breeder-owner Michele Perlmutter. An important Maltese who has made a fine show record.

Ch. Bar None Big Man On Campus, "Preppy" to his friends, in the
F.A.O. Schwartz store with his handler, Dee Shepherd. Michele
Perlmutter owns this stunning little dog.

Gladys Groskin was judging Teaneck when the Min Pin was shown under her and, placing him Reserve Winners, suggested that he would do better if his hind dewclaws were removed, which was done before his next show. The next show was at Trenton, where the author of this book was judging the large supported entry of the Eastern Miniature Pinscher Club. Michele's little dog was entered in Novice Class, which he won; then he went on to Winners Class, which he also won for five points. Michele, about twelve years old at the time, says, "I probably would have been more thrilled had I an idea at the time of what had just happened." But this was not all. The Min Pin, with his young owner handling, went on to Best of Breed over all the top Eastern Min Pins of that period, and Michele was completely convinced that dog shows are, indeed, a wonderful hobby. The Min Pin, Red Wrinkles, went on to complete his championship. But at that Trenton show, Michele saw the glamorous Maltese, Champion Co Ca He's Aennchen's Toy Dancer, owned by Anna Marie Stimmler, win the Toy Group there, and Michele completely lost her heart to Maltese that day.

Saving up her money in order to do so, Michele purchased a bitch puppy from Joanne Hesse (now one of her dearest friends). This one, Doll, never finished, but Michele's next one did, becoming Champion Joanne-Chen's Dancing Sheik. "Dolly" was bred to Sheik, giving Bar None its foundation bitch, Champion Bar None Scribble, who became the dam of eight puppies, six of which completed their American championships.

One of the latter was Champion Bar None Hot Rod Lincoln, whose sire was Champion Joanne-Chen's Square Dancer. A few years later Mrs. Hesse presented Square Dancer to Michele as a gift, but not before he had sired the Top Group-Winning Maltese of all time, Champion Joanne-Chen's Mino Maya Dancer. "Whitie," as Square Dancer was called, sired many more champions before he died of old age only a few months before this book was written.

Although with her limited breeding program Michele was never able to use "Linc" as much as she would have liked, he did sire about twenty puppies of which thirteen have become champions and others are en route to doing so. His progeny includes three Group-winners, two major-award winners, and a Best in Show dog.

Ch. Bar None Popeye with handler Tim Brazier. Michele Perlmutter, owner, Bar None Kennels, Ghent, New York.

Ch. Bar None Maggie Mae, one of the lovely Maltese owned by Michele Perlmutter, Ghent, New York.

Ch. Bar None Square Dancer, Michele Perlmutter, owner-handler.

Ch. Bar None Bette Davis Eyes is another Maltese owned by Michele Perlmutter, Ghent, New York.

At the latest American Maltese Association Specialty in Massachusetts in June 1983, Bar None The One and Only took Winners Bitch. She is a double granddaughter of "Linc," and she is the second Bar None Kizzy daughter to take the points at a National Specialty, the first having been Champion Bar None Sally May, a "Linc" daughter, who had been Best of Winners two years earlier. On that occasion her half-sister, Champion Bar None Electric Lady, went Best of Opposite Sex.

Although in recent years, Michele Perlmutter has used handlers for her dogs, she actually has finished the majority of them owner-handled. Now she is back doing it herself again almost entirely. As she comments, " I guess that might be called going full cycle."

Barnhill

Terence Childs and Joseph Champagne, of the Barnhill Kennels at Woodbury, Connecticut, both highly successful professional handlers, have been for years Maltese breeders as well.

It was back in the 1960's that they purchased a lovely Maltese, American and Canadian Champion Martin's Joker Puff, from Rena Martin, who did well for them both in the States and in Canada.

Now it is Champion Carlinda's Journey To All Star, owned by Joe Champagne, handled by him or by Terry Childs, with whom they have won Best in Show honors and multiple Groups. Journey To All Star is a widely admired, typey, very handsome son of Champion Carlinda's Latest Fashion ex Carlinda's Chatter Box, bred by Linda and Martin Di Giovanni.

Ch. Carlinda's Journey to all Star, a multiple Toy Group and all-breed Best in Show winner, owned and handled by Joseph R. Champagne, Barnhill Kennels, Woodbury, Conn., winning the Toy Group from Anna Katherine Nicholas at Putnam Kennel Club in 1982.

Am. and Can. Ch. Martin's Joker Puff, Group winner in the U.S. and Canada, finished title under George Fowler. Handled by Jane Lamarine and bred by Rena Martin. Owners Terence Childs and Joseph Champagne, Woodbury, Conn. This little Maltese is pictured at the Progressive Dog Club in 1969.

Ch. Jan-Don's Crystal Lady, finished in six shows, three of which were "majors," is a homebred belonging to Janet and Warren Orchard, Patchogue, New York. Handled by Terence Childs, P.H.A.

Bobb's

Bobb's Maltese are owned by Elaine Bobb at Chicago, Illinois, and are based on two excellent representatives of the finest possible bloodlines with which she has been working most successfully.

Champion Caramaya's Jorgy Boy is a winning son of Champion Caramaya's Bojangles (Champion Joanne-Chen's Maya Dancer ex Bayhammond's Tainie Dancer) ex Champion Maltes'a Joy (Champion Su-Le's Blue Jay ex Champion Cashmere's Maranna Dancer). Jorgy Boy, weighing four pounds, made his show debut at thirteen months of age, taking Best of Breed and a four-point major his first time in the ring.

Roath's Merri of Merriville, granddaughter of Champion Stentaway Drummer Boy and Champion Starward's Comet, herself a very handsome bitch, seems to be the perfect mate for Jorgy Boy judging by the quality puppies they have produced. Champion Bobb's Mae Wee J is a typical example of the quality of their offspring, as is Bobb's Melissa of Merri, currently being shown. Elaine Bobb's kennel is a small one but very select. A new litter soon due as this is written will be by Jorgy Boy from Bobb's Little Miss Boo, who is a half-sister to Merri and it is hoped she will produce equally well by Jorgy.

Bobb's Melissa J of Merri, a daughter of Ch. Caramaya's Jorgy Boy, is being shown as we go to press with points toward the title. Owned by Elaine Bobb, Chicago, Illinois.

Bee Bee Doll J is a daughter of Ch. Caramaya's Jorgy Boy and litter sister to Ch. Bobb's Mae Wee J. With points towards her title, she is owned by Elaine Bobb, Chicago, Illinois.

Ch. Bobb's Mae Wee J. handled by Jo Ann Dinsmore, gained the title in no time flat for owner, Elaine Bobb, Chicago, Illinois. By Ch. Caramaya's Jorgy Boy ex Roath's Merri of Merrivale.

Chelsea

Chelsea Maltese belong to Gail Hennessey at Wappinger Falls, New York, who is a devoted enthusiast of this breed. Champion Kathan's Blu Flower of Chelsea was Gail's first one to finish, which she did in 1979. Bred by Linda and Nick Kenny, of Hopelawn, New Jersey, "Lily" made some exciting wins as she gained her championship. She then went on to obedience school and maternal duties, emerging from the latter as the dam of Ms. Hennessey's first homebred to finish, Champion Danny's Jude of Chelsea, named for St. Jude (Patron of the Impossible) and the entertainer, Danny Thomas. "Dee Jaay," as this little dog is called, now resides in Oklahoma with Mrs. Shirley Sherwood. He is a son of Champion Kathan's Peppermint Stick from Champion Kathan's Blu Flower of Chelsea and was just twelve months old when he completed his title.

Left, Ch. Kathan's Bluflower of Chelsea with her son, Ch. Danny's Jude of. Chelsea. Both owned by Gail Hennessey, Chelsea Kennels, Wappinger Falls, New York.

Oak Ridge Ciara, with 3 points towards title, bred by Carol Neth, who until recently has co-owned her with Gail Hennessey.

There are other very special Maltese in Gail Hennessey's life, in addition to these as, for example, the one she refers to as her "companion Maltese," Chelsea's Merry Andrew, and his dam, Chelsea's Little Daisy. Also there is Su-Le's American Goldfinch which was part of Ms. Hennessey's family for awhile who is now returned—Gail hopes only temporarily—to stay with her breeder, Barbara Bergquist, until Gail is again in a position to keep more Maltese than she can keep at the present time.

This famous Best in Show winner is Ch. Joanne-Chen's Maja Dancer, owner-handled to many important victories by Jo Ann Dinsmore, Arlington Heights, Illinois.

Jo Ann

Jo Ann's Maltese, at Arlington Heights, Illinois, started in 1964 when Mrs. Jo Ann Dinsmore made the purchase of her first member of the breed, promptly becoming captivated by the loving bright personality of these little white dogs. Her first champion was bred by Mary Hechinger and finished in both Canada and the United States, Champion Stentaway Sonny Boy.

Mrs. Dinsmore was able to purchase several good bitches from the Joanne-Chen line. Two of these, Joanne-Chen's Maja Dancer and Joanne-Chen's Melodee Dancer became the foundation of her breeding program which is producing outstandingly beautiful type and quality dogs. Champion Maja, specialed only four times, won Best in Show, then was retired for matronly duties.

Champion Jo Ann's Majestic Minstrel Man was the first homebred of Mrs. Dinsmore's to gain championship honors.

The current winner at Jo Ann's as this is written is the widely admired Champion Jo Ann's Merrylane Matchmaker (Champion Tumblemere's Beau Jester ex Champion Debbie's Majestic Crysta Lyn), who through 1982 had gained the show record of seventy-five times Best of Breed, eight times Best Toy, twelve Group seconds, nine Group thirds, and twelve Group fourths.

Ch. Jo Ann's Majestic Minstrel Man (right, wearing bows) with his mother, Joanne-Chen's Melodee Dancer. Jo Ann Dinsmore, owner, Arlington Heights, Illinois.

Jo Ann Dinsmore with her daughter Carrie Dinsmore and judge Merrill Cohen. Here Ch. Merrylane Matchmaker (left) is pictured with his son, Ch. Maltesa Royal Match, Matchmaker taking Best of Breed as Royal Match completes his championship with Best of Winners. Both owned by Jo Ann Dinsmore, Arlington Heights, Illinois.

Ch. Jo Ann's Merrylane Matchmaker, by Ch. Tumblemere's Beau Jester ex Ch. Debbie's Majestic Crysta Lynn, bred, owned and handled by Jo Ann Dinsmore, Arlington Heights, Illinois, has the imposing record of 43 Group placements (including 8 Group Firsts) from 75 Bests of Breed. A very nice accomplishment.

He is an owner-handled homebred and is already making worthwhile contributions as a sire. In his first litter he sired three males, all of whom became champions. And he has four other champions to his credit, along with numerous youngsters currently in competition with points toward their titles.

Jo Ann's Maltese are intelligent as well as beautiful, and Mrs. Dinsmore takes pride in being the breeder of the Top Obedience Maltese for 1980, 1981, and 1982, Champion Ginger Jake, U.D. and Canadian C.D.X., who was the first obedience winner in the National Maltese Specialty. He is trained and owned by Faith Ann Maciejewski of West Allis, Wisconsin.

Kathan

Kathan's Maltese belong to Kathy Di Giacomo at Fair Lawn, New Jersey, who has been extremely successful as a breeder-exhibitor of some truly excellent dogs.

I first met Kathy in 1977 when she was showing a promising puppy, Kathan's Delta Dawn. Since then I have seen her with many exceptionally nice homebreds.

Kathan's is the home of a fast rising young star among Maltese sires, Champion Kathan's Sunshine Superman, who numbers among his progeny such lovely Maltese as Champion Su-Le's Mynah II (a bitch who is doing considerable winning for Kathy Di Giacomo and Elyse R. Fischer of Port Washington, New

We love this photo of Ch. Kathan's Tangerine, bred, owned and handled by Kathy Di Giacomo of Fair Lawn, New Jersey, taking "winners" at Greater Philadelphia in 1982. Left to right, Kathy's daughter Stefanie Di Giacomo, the judge Merrill Cohen, Tangerine, and Kathy.

In the early days of Kathan's Maltese, this lovely 9-month puppy, Kathan's Delta Dawn, was one of the first to complete championship title. Owner-handled by Kathy Di Giacomo.

Ch. Su-Le's Mynah II belongs to Elyse R. Fischer and Kathy Di Giacomo, and is taking Best of Breed at Greater Philadelphia in 1982.

Kathan's Torquay of Toyland, breeder-owner handled by Kathy Di Giacomo, co-bred with Peg Vicedomini.

York), Champion Kathan's Layla of Viceroy, Champion Su-Le's Purple Martin, Champion Louan's Cherokee Sunshine, Champion Su-Le's Motmot, and Champion Su-Le's Star Finch.

Champion Kathan's Tangerine is an owner-handled homebred; Viceroy Kathan's Honeycomb should be finished by now, bred by Kathy Di Giacomo and owned by Laura Ford. Kathan's Torquey of Toyland, co-bred by Kathy Di Giacomo and Peg Vicedomini, is being handled successfully by Kathy; and the owner-handled-homebred Su-Le's Atlantic Brent is another making his presence felt.

Then there is Kathan's Blue Image, by Champion Su-Le's Bluebird from Su-Le's Linnet, bred by Kathy who co-owns him with Alfreda M. Riley. Kathan's April Love, a daughter of Champion Kathan's Lavender Blue, is owned by Kathy with M. Greenburg. Su-Le's Caribea, by the breed's top sire, Champion To The Victor of Eng, is co-owned by Kathy and Elyse Fischer. Champion Kathan's Rhinestone Cowboy is siring winners. And there are numerous others who have brought credit to this kennel and its owner. Kathy Di Giacomo is a talented breeder, and it would seem that Kathan's Maltese will be making an impression on the Maltese world for generations to come.

Krystal

Krystal Maltese are located at Glendale Heights, Illinois, and are owned by Kristine Collins who is a fairly new breeder having joined the Maltese Fancy during the late 1970's. She has been a successful one, however, and is off to a good start with some very lovely dogs.

Ms. Collins has some definite ideas about what is important to her breeding program; and as a result of putting her ideas into practice, she has several excellent producing bitches. More than by pedigree, she is guided by the quality of the individual dog, always looking for the soundest animal she can find. She places special emphasis on free whelpers, not believing in Caesarean sections as a matter of course but only if absolutely necessary to save the life of the mother.

Among the Maltese at Krystal Kennels is the handsome little "Elvis," more formally known as Tampier's Love Me Tender, with some good wins to his credit. Since she became "hooked" on this breed with the first one she met, Ms. Collins has ambitious plans for the future and is planning to devote considerable time to her Maltese breeding program.

This is Star, owned by Krystal Maltese, Glendale Heights, Illinois.

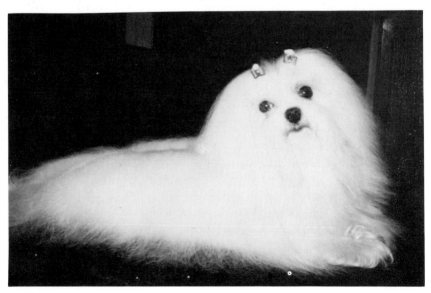

Tampier's Love Me Tender is among the winning Maltese at Krystal Kennels owned by Kris Collins, Glendale Heights, Illinois.

Ch. Joanne-Chen's Teddy Bear in 1968. Marcia Hostetter, owner, Des Moines, Iowa.

March'en

The March'en Maltese belong to Marcia Hostetter of Des Moines, Iowa, who maintains them purely as a hobby, and have been marching around the show rings since 1964. The first ones were not very pretty by today's standards according to Mrs. Hostetter, and so she studied and observed as she garnered reserves awards, her final decision being that she liked, wanted, and needed dogs of the Aennchen type on which to base her breeding program. Aennchen Antonelli was contacted, and it was from her that Mrs. Hostetter received the suggestion to get in touch with Joanne Hesse, who had at that time recently moved from the East to Fort Wayne, Indiana, as her Joanne-Chen dogs were based on Aennchen's, and from Mrs. Hesse she would find

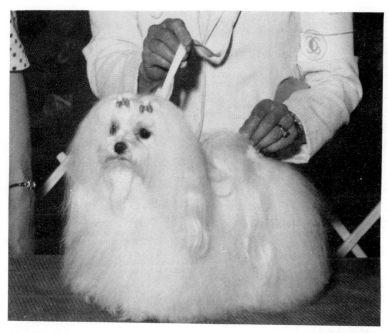

Ch. March'en Kewpie Dancer going Best of Winners under Iris de la Torre Bueno, owner-handled by Marcia Hostetter, March'en Maltese, Des Moines, Iowa.

top representations of these combined great bloodlines. Marcia Hostetter did so, and thus it was that Champion Joanne-Chen's Teddy Bear Dancer became the first Aennchen/Joanne-Chen dog west of the Mississippi.

Teddy Bear, his first time in the ring as a Special, won the Toy Group from Jim Trullinger and was a strong contender that day under Clark Thompson for Best in Show. Out of three times entered as a Special, Teddy Bear twice won the Group and probably would have built up quite a spectacular record had Mrs. Hostetter really campaigned him. But she was interested principally in breeding a few good ones, showing them herself, and then enjoying them as family companions to be loved and admired. All but two of the Maltese she has shown, or placed in show homes, have had Group placements from the classes, which is a source of satisfaction to her.

The March'en breeding program has always been based on line-breeding, with the exception of just two "outside" breedings which turned out to be disappointments so far as Mrs. Hostetter

WINNERS BITCH
LAND O' LAKES K.C.
JUNE 8, 1975
OLSON PHOTO

March'en Bali Dancer, by Ch. March'en Martini Dancer ex Joanne-Chen's Mini Maid Dancer, pictured winning a "major" with her owner-handler Marcia Hostetter, Des Moines, Iowa.

was concerned. Her chief goal in breeding is to produce type, disposition, soundness, and correct size; and she takes pride that litters raised at March'en have included those of multiple champions. Marcia Hostetter does not breed bitches which have not completed their championships, and she does not sell her puppies before they have reached four to six months of age.

Many of the early March'en Maltese carried the Joanne-Chen/Aennchen prefix, and Mrs. Hostetter takes pride in the fact that her Maltese have the heritage of these famous and beautiful dogs. The March'en logo of marching Maltese—one she has treasured over the years—was done for her as a gift by Tony Antonelli.

Martin's (Marjorie)

Marjorie Martin, owner of Martin's Maltese at Columbus, Ohio, acquired her first member of the breed during the early 1970's. Since that time her dogs have been highly successful, and the results of her breeding program, based on a son and two granddaughters of the noted Champion Maltacello El-Cid, are a credit to her talents as a breeder.

The El-Cid son is Champion Martin's Michael-Cid, handled to his championship, as was El-Cid, by Barbara Alderman. The two granddaughters are Michael's Cookie and Chris's Sugar.

Ch. Martin's Chanel-Cid handled here by Barbara Alderman for Marjorie Martin, Columbus, Ohio.

WINNERS

GREATER DAYTONA
DOG FANCIERS ASSN.
JANUARY 1983

Graham PHOTO BY SABRINA

These Maltese beauties are, left, Ch. Martin's Rachel-Cid and, right, Ch. Martin's Foxwel-Cid, both by Ch. Martin's Michael-Cid ex Michael's Cookie, bred, owned, and handled by David Martin and Marjorie Martin, Martin's Maltese, Columbus, Ohio.

Cookie is the dam, by Michael, of the exquisite Champion Michael's Chanel-Cid, Champion Martin's Rachel-Cid, and others. Sugar, with Michael, produced Champion Martin's Christel-Cid and Champion Martin's Annabel-Cid. Others from this combination of line-breeding include Champion Martin's Foxwel-Cid and Champion Martin's Maxwel-Cid.

At Barbara Alderman's suggestion, the lovely bitch Champion Martin's Chanel-Cid was bred to the dog she has been campaigning, Champion Noble Faith's Charmin Fella. The results are really exciting, as there is a puppy in the six-week-old litter over which Marjorie Martin is really enthusiastic.

We note, and admire, the obviously good sound structure of Mrs. Martin's dogs, their pretty little faces, short backs, and straight legs. As a Maltese breeder, she obviously is doing a great deal right!

Rena and Daryl Martin's

Rena Martin and her family have been involved as breeders with Maltese since 1959 at their kennel in Highland Park, Illinois.

Among the early winners here, Champion Martin's Flopsy Puff (Chota Manu Burra Kama Rama ex Cacciatori of Villa Malta) finished his title in ten shows under nine different judges and became a Group winner his first time out as a Special. He and Champion Martin's Candida (a half-sister from the same Villa Malta dam) formed the first Best in Show Brace owned by

Ch. Martin's Jingles Puff, a Top Winning Maltese dog owned by Rena Martin, Highland Park, Illinois. A Best in Show winner, this little dog had numerous exciting victories to his credit during the late 1960s and early 1970s.

Rena Martin and handled by her then teen-age daughter, Daryl. She won Best Brace in Show with them on at least two occasions and Best Toy Brace numerous times, including the big Chicago-International. Later this brace was replaced by Champion Martin's Jingles Puff and Champion Martin's Bangles Puff, littermates by Mike Mar's Dazzling Dancer ex Martin's Sparkle Puff, who won Best Toy Brace at Westminster in 1969 and many other exciting and prestigious awards for their talented young handler.

Rena's breeding program goes back to Villa Malta, Mike Mar, and Aennchen, among other quality dogs, and has been extremely successful, both for her and for providing the fine quality which her clients have used advantageously in their own kennels.

Rena Martin had been a Puli breeder for years, President of the Puli Club of America for four years, and was writing the *Gazette* column on the breed when she decided that she would like to have a Toy breed. Maltese were her selection as they "reminded her of Pulik in appearance." Her career as a professional handler got underway when she discovered that she could find no one to show the Maltese for her who could do so and keep the dogs' coats. Thus she started handling her own dogs; she eventually became a professional, showing and finishing many Maltese for many clients.

Daryl apprenticed under her mother, having grown up with a deep love for and interest in dogs. In fact the entire Martin family shares this feeling and the involvement with dogs. Rena has an exclusive grooming salon in addition to her handling activities; husband Marty has a dog motel and pet shop; and daughter Daryl, who started out at a very early age training puppies to the lead and caring for the house dogs, is now one of the country's leading handlers, with a particular flair for the small "coated" breeds.

Since the Martins, almost from the beginning, have been professional handlers, it has been impossible for them to campaign dogs of their own, feeling that their clients must get first preference. But they enjoy the fruits of their success as they see descendants of their dogs doing well for their clients and as they finish champions and make record-building wins for them.

When she earned the Quaker Oats Award in 1981 for Number One Toy Dog with Blanche Tenerowicz's Champion Joanne-Chen's Mino Maya Dancer, Daryl became the youngest person to ever gain this honor.

A multiple Best in Show winner of the 1960s, Ch. Martin's Jingles Puff owned and handled by Rena Martin, Highland Park, Illinois.

Ch. Martin's Koko Bean Puff, by Ch. Martin's Sweet Bean Puff, was bred and handled by Rena and Daryl Martin for Blanche Tenerowicz, Easthampton, Mass.

BEST OF WINNERS
INDIANHEAD K.C.
DEC. 12, 1982
OLSON PHOTO

Oak Ridge

Oak Ridge Maltese, at McMurray, Pennsylvania, had their start in 1964 with the purchase by Carol A. and Tom Neth of a bitch, Koukla Lady of Rhodes, from Gini Sunner of Maltacello Maltese. Koukla combined Good Time, Invicta, and Aennchen breeding and later became the foundation of Carol Neth's breeding stock.

While raising her children, Carol Neth had little time for dog shows. She was, however, then attending a grooming school taught by Shirley Kalstone. It was while working in a grooming salon owned by Gini Sunner that she learned much about the earlier Maltese bloodlines, the actual grooming, and also had the opportunity to study structure and movement of many breeds, all of which have been helpful to her as a breeder-exhibitor. To this day she still enjoys her vocation as a professional all-breed groomer.

At first the Neths' Maltese used the prefix Bali Hai; and when Koukla was bred for the first time, to Champion Duncan's Kimberley, she produced for them Bali Hai's Misty Pebbles.

In 1969, the Neths acquired their own stud dog, Champion Infante's Mystic Caper, from Mr. and Mrs. Alan Rhodes, a dog bred by Rose Infante. This little dog proved an excellent sire and was still producing at age thirteen until his death in 1980. He "nicked" nicely with Misty Pebbles to produce the Neths' first homebred Best in Show winner, Champion Oak Ridge Melissa, and later the great American, Canadian, and Bermudian Champion Oak Ridge Country Charmer, along with numerous other champions. The last by him were Champion Oak Ridge Country 'n Lace and Champion Oak Ridge Country Caper, born after his death.

During 1970, Carol Neth started sending her dogs out to shows with Evelyn Schaeffer of Evo-Ron's Kennel in Cortland, Ohio. They became close friends, and Carol credits this lady with having taught her much about the breed. Evelyn Schaeffer finished Champion Oak Ridge Pufnstuff at nine and a half months of age with four majors and two Bests of Breed from the classes. His owner describes him as "a cobby, baby-faced little male who became one of Oak Ridge's best producers." One of his "kids," now carrying on for him, is a son, Champion Oak Ridge Poppin Fresh, from a Country Charmer sister, Oak Ridge Sand Pebble. Evelyn Schaeffer later purchased Champion Evo-

A moment's relaxation for famous Best in Show winner, Am., Can. and Bda. Ch. Oak Ridge Country Charmer owned by Carol A. and Tom Neth, Oak Ridge Maltese, McMurray, Pennsylvania.

Ch. Oak Ridge Feather Duster finished her title under Mr. Tipton. Carol A. Neth handled.

Ron's Jendi from Oak Ridge whom she finished and dearly loved. Following this lady's death in 1981, Jendi returned to Oak Ridge along with her daughter and her granddaughter.

In 1975, Carol Neth began showing Bali Hai's Lil Pebbles and Oak Ridge Lil Miss Sunshine, who became her first breeder-owner-handled champions. Then along came an individual who from earliest puppyhood seemed destined for greatness, born in February 1975, who was named Oak Ridge Country Charmer. He gained his American championship with Best of Breed and Group placements from the classes (then cheered on his litter-sister, Champion Oak Ridge Country Luv, to hers), piled up a whole list of thrilling honors in Canada where he quickly made a bit of history, and took on Bermuda in the same style to become a triple-title holder, an American, Canadian, and Bermudian champion.

When Charmer completed his show career, at the Western Reserve Kennel Club event in December 1980 by winning the Toy Group there, he had amassed an amazing number of noteworthy victories with a record which stands as follows: 237 Bests of Breed, twenty-three Bests in Show, ninety-two firsts in Group, one hundred additional Group placements, championships in three countries, twice Best of Breed at the National Specialty (first Maltese *dog* to achieve this), Best of Breed at Westminster, Best in Show at Montreal International, and, the true "frosting on the cake," breeder-owner-handled all the way!

Charmer has now settled down to a life of retirement, basking in the reflected glory of the success his sons and daughters are having in the ring. At the close of 1982, there were fifteen champions to his credit, and he points with particular pride to his multi-Best in Show and Group-winning daughter, Best in Show at the 1983 National Specialty and Best of Breed at Westminster the same year, Champion Noble Faith's White Tornado, owned by Faith Knoble of Miami, Florida, and handled by Barbara Alderman. Faith Knoble also owns a Charmer son, Champion Noble Faith's Charmin Fella.

In 1981, along with finishing Champion Oak Ridge Poppin' Fresh on the Florida Circuit, Carol also finished Champion Mystique's Country Charmin' for Donna and David Perret of Pensacola. This breeding was later repeated, producing Champion Oak Ridge Dust Buster. Champion Oak Ridge Sweet Memory has also been doing well, as has the Charmer son,

Ch. Oak Ridge Justa Charm, by Ch. Oak Ridge Country Charmer ex Oak Ridge Lil' White Dove. Handled by Carol Neth.

Left, Ch. Oak Ridge Portrait of Puff handled by Wendy Neth. Right, Ch. Oak Ridge Country Charmer handled by Carol Neth. A family portrait of charm and beauty!

The foundation behind the Oak Ridge Maltese. Ch. Infante's Mystic Caper (top), the sire of many fine champions including Am., Can., Bda. Ch. Oak Ridge Country Charmer; and Koukla Lady of Rhodes (bottom), the Neths' foundation bitch, producer of Bali Hai's (Oak Ridge) Misty Pebbles, the dam of 2 Best in Show Maltese and many other champions. Carol A. and Tom Neth, owners, McMurray, Pennsylvania.

Champion Oak Ridge Risin Shine, owned by the Graffs from Louisiana and handled by Mr. Graff and by Peggy Lloyd.

Champion Oak Ridge Illusive Dream finished in short order, as did Champion Oak Ridge Free Spirit, who is owned and loved by Elsie Westrope in Canada. Champion Oak Ridge Winn Dixie became the last daughter to finish by Champion Oak Ridge Pufnstuf, and Champion Oak Ridge Country Heather, by Champion Oak Ridge Justa Charm ex Champion Oak Ridge Sweet Alyssum, completed title for Diane Davis of Florida.

Ch. Oak Ridge Winn Dixie winning the breed for Carol Neth at Pocono Mountain in 1981.

Ch. Oak Ridge Sugar Pop, by Ch. Oak Ridge Poppin Fresh ex Oak Ridge Sand Pebble, bred, owned, and handled by Carol A. Neth, McMurray, Pennsylvania.

Am., Can., Bda. Ch. Oak Ridge Country Charmer winning his second American Maltese Association National Specialty, Sept. 1979. Mr. Merrill Cohen, judge. Carol Neth, breeder-owner-handler.

By 1982 Champion Oak Ridge Poppin Fresh had reached the producing age, and now numbers among his progeny Champion Oak Ridge Sugar Pop and Champion Oak Ridge Crispy Critter, both bred and handled by Carol. Crispy, upon becoming a champion, was sold to a fancier in Japan where his influence on the breed should be a good one. Champion Wesglyn Kool Pop did well for Glynette Cass. And George McIntosh, upon becoming interested in the breed, flew to Oak Ridge where, from among four bitches offered, selected his beautiful Champion Oak Ridge East Side Wonder, now winning well for him.

There is another champion in the Neth household, their daughter Wendy, who is the youngest of their three girls. This young lady was written up in the November-December 1982 issue of *Maltese Tales* as the featured Junior Handler, having been the Top Junior Handler in Maltese for 1979, 1980, and 1981. Wendy began helping her mother show dogs (and attending Beagle field trials with her dad) at a very early age. Her love for both Maltese and Beagles keeps her torn between the two rings, and she can be seen in Junior Handling with either breed. In 1980, she was Number One in Maltese and Number Two Nationally, alternating between several Maltese and her Beagles.

Pegden

The Pegden Kennels of Peggy Lloyd and Denny Mounce at Houston, Texas, originated in June of 1975. Peggy had been breeding Maltese since 1968 under the Valley High prefix. Denny was new to the breed but had been raising and showing Dachshunds since 1970.

Using Peggy's Valley High bitches, which were primarily of Aennchen breeding, a small breeding program was begun. With both Peggy and Denny committed to their handling careers, they were limited at first to raising only one or two litters each year.

Pegden's foundation bitch was American and Canadian Champion Valley High Sugar Cookie, who was ranked Number Ten Maltese at that time. In 1977, they purchased American, Mexican, and International Champion Mac's Apache Joray of Everon. "Danny" had been bred by Evelyn Schaefer and was then a young class dog. Peggy and Denny finished him undefeated and were proud of the fact that he had the qualities they consider essential to breeding good Maltese. Although they

Amer., Mex., Int. Ch. Mac's Apache Joray of Everon, a Maltese Merit Award Sire, proudly owned by Peggy Lloyd and Denny Mounce, Pegden Kennels.

Ch. Valley High First Mate belongs to Peggy Lloyd and Denny Mounce of the Pegden Kennels in Sugar Land, Texas. Denny Mounce took this exquisite headstudy photo.

Amer. and Can. Ch. Valley High Sugar Cookie is one of the handsome Maltese at Pegden Kennels, Peggy Lloyd and Denny Mounce, Sugar Land, Texas. Photo by Rae Eckes.

had always bred for sound, five- to five-and-a-half-pound Maltese, he was the turning point in their dogs, his contributions having been great. "Danny" stamped his puppies, right from the first, with the qualities his owners were seeking, including the beautiful heads and strong, straight white coats so desired and admired by his owners.

From time to time, Pegden has introduced an occasional outcross to top winning dogs, but they actually prefer the results of line-breeding. Every bitch at Pegden is bred with the intention to produce *better* dogs, and they feel it important to breed dogs that complement one another rather than base the breeding on pedigrees alone.

Rebecca's

Rebecca's Maltese, owned by Mrs. Freda Tinsley of Scottsdale, Arizona, are the perfect answer to those who say one must have a huge kennel operation in order to breed winners. This kennel is small and very exclusive, yet Mrs. Tinsley is breeding an impressive array of top quality dogs who are succeeding extremely well in competition, including the Number One Maltese in the United States for 1981 and 1982, Champion Rebecca's Desert Valentino, who is also the Number Two Toy Dog for 1982 and Number Twenty-two among all breeds for 1982. "Val" has won the National Specialty; he has numerous Bests in Show to his credit (including three out of four on a recent Mission Circuit); and he has very many Toy Group firsts. He certainly is an impressive little dog who has brought pride to his breed and to the Maltese Fancy!

Mrs. Tinsley's active participation in the Maltese world started back during the late 1960's when she purchased one which was actually intended to be a pet.

The first of Mrs. Tinsley's homebreds to become a champion was Rebecca's Desert Angel and as she says, finishing this first one was an unforgettable thrill. Desert Angel really did it the right way, too, gaining championship from the Puppy Classes and going on to Best of Breed over Specials.

Rebecca's Maltese are a true family project. Named for the Tinsleys' only child, Rebecca, both Freda Tinsley and her husband, Ted, are much involved with the dogs, as is Rebecca, and enjoy nothing more than all getting into the ring at the same time and competing against one another. Rebecca started in Junior Showmanship when she was eight years old, and by the time she was sixteen, she had won the National Specialty with Champion So Big's Desert Delight (Champion Rebecca's Desert So Big ex Codere's D.D.'s Delight) and won an all-breed Best in Show under Mrs. Thelma Brown. Rebecca, at age fifteen, also started her own grooming shop, Rebecca's Magic Clippers, and still grooms dogs as well as being a licensed hairdresser—the latter "carrying on in the family tradition," as Freda herself owns a highly successful hairdressing salon. Ted Tinsley also is doing grooming—all of which adds up to a very compatible family.

A delightful pose of Ch. Rebecca's Desert Valentino done by Missy Yuhl for the Tinsleys, owners of this Maltese, Number One for the breed in America, 1981 and 1982.

Ch. Rebecca's Desert Valentino, destined to become Number One for the breed in 1981 and 1982, photographed on the day he gained his first Best of Breed after completing his championship.

Ch. Rebecca's Desert Mr. Delight, by Rebecca's Desert Angel Boy ex Ch. So Big's Desert Delight, is a half-brother to Valentino and himself the sire of some fine champions. Mrs. Freda Tinsley owner, Scottsdale, Arizona.

This is Ch. Rebecca's Living Doll, a litter sister to Ch. Rebecca's Pretty Girl. Doll is proving an outstanding producer, judging by her puppies by Valentino which will soon be in the ring.

This tiny charmer, Ch. So Big's Desert Delight, by Ch. Rebecca's Desert So Big ex Codere's D-D's Delight, shown by Rebecca Tinsley is winning the 1976 American Maltese Association National Specialty under judge Mrs. Ann Stevenson.

As a Junior Handler, Rebecca won many Best in Junior Showmanship awards while showing her Champion Rebecca's Desert Love, who is the grandmother of Valentino.

In her breeding program, Freda Tinsley places particular emphasis on the importance of good movement, straight top lines, and nice head carriage, all enhanced by nice straight coats; and she feels, too, that correct black pigmentation is a feature which should be emphasized and kept in mind by both breeders and judges.

Valentino is retired now from the ring and is proving himself an outstanding sire. There will be some lovely descendants of this great dog in competition for a long time to come, who will surely add distinguished further honors to those already gained by the Tinsley-bred Maltese.

Ch. Russ Ann the Gentle Touch, by Ch. Russ Ann Mr. Pip ex Ch. Russ Ann Repeat Performance, bred by Anna Mae Hardy and handled by Michael Wolf, co-owner with David Fitzpatrick.

Ch. Russ Ann Petite Charmer, owned by Anna Mae J. Hardy, during an 8-month show career was winner of 2 Bests in Show, an All Toy Show, 10 Group Firsts, and 25 additional Group placements to become # 2 Maltese and # 1 Maltese Bitch for 1974, *Kennel Review* System. Additionally, Charm is the Top Producing Best in Show Maltese Bitch of all time, and in 1979 was awarded the *Kennel Review* Silver Certificate as a Top Producer.

Russ Ann

When Russ Ann Maltese were established, Anna Mae Hardy of Floral City, Florida, had never owned a purebred dog and had never even heard of dog shows. It all came about through her across-the-street-neighbor, in whose yard Mrs. Hardy noticed what she thought was a cat playing. Being allergic to cats, she paid no attention *until* she was told that the little animal was a Maltese dog, not a cat, and that this neighbor raised them. It was only a short time later that Anna Mae Hardy had her first Maltese on a lease deal with Joyce Watkins of Marcris Maltese, to whom the first litter went in payment for the bitch.

The second litter brought Mrs. Hardy her first champion, Gidget of Marcris, who she showed and finished herself. The

Alert in the show ring, Ch. Russ Ann A Touch of Class owned by Ann Hardy, Floral City, Florida.

third litter gave her another champion, Bobbelee Tammy Tu of Marcris, by which time she was thoroughly "hooked" on the fun of owning Maltese and of showing her own dogs.

With the responsibility of a growing family at home, Mrs. Hardy was not always able to make as many shows as she would have enjoyed. But she put the time at home to good use where her dogs were concerned, by perfecting the art of grooming and of putting up topknots, which she now teaches many others, realizing that grooming and conditioning is a fine art.

Mrs. Hardy brought home the puppy who would become Champion Russ Anne Petite Charmer when she was still very much of a novice and Charm was only eight weeks old. Charm's first win came at three months of age when she was entered in an All-Breed Fun Match where she won Best Toy.

In February 1972, Charm and Mrs. Hardy set off for Chicago, to the American Maltese Association National Specialty, held in conjunction with the International. Charm was just six months old, and when she beat twenty-six puppies to gain Best Puppy in Sweepstakes, Mrs. Hardy was really flying. Charm completed her championship at ten and a half months of age, taking most of her points from the Puppy and Bred-by-Exhibitor Classes. Her owner continued showing her as a Special, winning Best of Breed many times but no Group placements. And so it was decided to try her with a professional handler. John Thyssen was selected for this assignment, and she returned with him to New Mexico following Westminster in 1974. During eight months of campaigning, Charm's record grew to include two all-breed Bests in Show, one Toy Best in Show, ten firsts in the Toy Group, thirteen Group seconds, nine Group thirds, and three Group fourths. She ended up Number One Maltese *bitch* and Number Two Maltese, *Kennel Review* System, for that year.

Mrs. Hardy describes August 13th, 1973 as one of the most exciting days she ever recalls. There was a new type of dog show held in Stone Mountain, Georgia, on that day, an all-breed competition for the National Kennel Pageant which included only four southern states. For breed and group, each judge had a ballot to score the handler and dog in ten categories. The wins were all on a point system, a total of three judges' ballots determining the first, second, and third; a total of six judges to determine the Group awards; and a total of nine judges for Best in

Ch. Russ Ann A Touch of Class, by Ch. Coeur De Lion ex Ch. Russ Ann Petite Charmer, is a Best in Show winner and for 2 years was #7 Maltese in the United States. Anna Mae Hardy, breeder-owner, Russ Ann Kennels, Floral City, Florida.

Mutual admiration! Anna Mae Hardy of Floral City, Florida, with her famous Best in Show winning Ch. Russ Ann Petite Charmer, Top Maltese bitch and Number 2 Maltese, 1974 *Kennel Review* System.

Show. Charm wound up the Best in Show, making it an occasion which Mrs. Hardy will never forget.

In 1975, Charm produced her first litter, which included Champion Russ Ann Bonus Baby and Champion Russ Ann Mr. Pip, these by Champion C. and M.'s Valentino of Midhill. Her next breeding, to Champion Coeur De Lion, produced Champion Russ Ann A Touch of Class, Number Seven Maltese in the United States for two years and a Best in Show dog. The next breeding was a repeat to Coeur De Lion, producing two more champions, Jaydora's Scarlet Touch and Russ Ann A Touch of Charm. The next breeding was a repeat of the first time, to Champion C. and M.'s Valentino of Midhill, which contained Champion Gordon's Legend of Russ Ann owned by Pauline Clarke. "Rusty" has several Group wins to his credit and, now residing in Switzerland with Jacques and Renate Aubort, has become a Swiss and International champion.

Charm's next and final breeding was to Champion Caramaya's Mister; the result was two girls, one finished (Champion Russ Anne Repeat Performance) and the other pointed.

In 1979, Mrs. Hardy took Charm to the National Specialty in Houston, Texas, where she was entered in the Veterans Class, being then seven years old. To her owner's delight, Charm took the class, then went on to Best of Opposite Sex over seventeen champion bitches. This was the icing on the cake for Mrs. Hardy with this great bitch, who is now retired from both the show ring and the whelping box and rules the roost as the special house pet at Russ Ann!

Mrs. Hardy is probably even prouder of Charm's success as a producer than she is of her show record, for it, too, is very exceptional. To the best of her knowledge Charm is the Top Producing Best in Show Maltese Bitch of all time. And she is the winner of the *Kennel Review* Silver Certificate as a Top Producer in 1979.

Seventeen of Mrs. Hardy's dogs have completed their championships as this book is written, with four of Russ Ann breeding presently competing in the show ring. Pauline Clarke is going to Switzerland to show Champion Gordon's Legend of Russ Ann in the World Championship Show at Madrid, Spain. If he attains a world championship title, he will be the only American-bred Maltese to have accomplished this achievement.

In breeding Charm, Mrs. Hardy used only Top Producer studs.

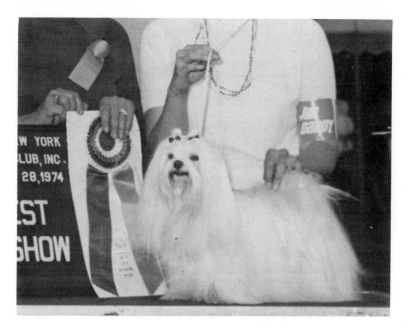

Am., Can. and Bda. Ch. Mike Mar's My Twilight Dream (Sabrina), by Ch. Mike Mar's Devil Dancer ex Mike Mar's Witch Doctor, was bred by Michael Wolf and is owned by Marcia Richardson, Sabrina Maltese, Christiana, Pennsylvania. Winning Best in Show at Central New York in 1974, Sabrina also boasts several Canadian Bests in Show and was Best of Breed Maltese at Westminster 1974.

Sabrina

Sabrina Maltese were established in April of 1971 when Marcia Richardson, now of Christiana, Pennsylvania, saw a Maltese for the first time. She had long owned Cocker Spaniels and Yorkshire Terriers, but these little white dogs truly won her heart—a real case of love at first sight!

Sabrina, for whom the kennel is named, was Marcia Richardson's first Maltese. She was purchased from Michael Wolf, her full name being Champion Mike Mar's My Twilight Dream, and she went on to become an American, Canadian, and Bermudian champion. Her victories included a Best in Show in the United States and several in Canada. And she also won the breed at Westminster in 1974. Bred by Michael Wolf, Sabrina is a daughter of Champion Mike Mar's Devil Dancer ex Mike Mar's 'Witch Doctor. As this is written, in 1983, Sabrina is thoroughly enjoying life at thirteen years of age.

113

Sabrina's Star Kissed Cherub, great-granddaughter of Am. Can., Bda. Ch. Villa Malta's Kimba and Am., Can., Bda. Ch. Mike Mar's My Twilight Dream at 9 months taking Best of Breed from the classes in a 4-point "major." Marcia Richardson, breeder-owner-handler, Sabrina Kennels, Christiana, Pennsylvania.

American, Canadian, and Bermudian Champion Villa Malta's Kimba, by Nugett of Villa Malta ex Maryette of Villa Malta, was bred by Marge Rozik from whom Marcia Richardson purchased him. He is completely Villa Malta bred and has done well for her both in the show ring and as a producer.

Sabrina's Star Kissed Cherub is the great granddaughter of Kimba and Sabrina. Her first time in the ring, at only eight months of age, she won Best of Breed from the Puppy Class over Specials. She is Sabrina's My O My Alfred from Sabrina's Especially Me and is a homebred.

Marcia Richardson breeds between one and six litters annually, working mainly with the "old" Mike Mar line and the Villa Malta line with some Revlo crossed in, which adds up to a solid combination of Aennchen, Jo Aennchen, and Villa Malta, certainly providing outstanding background for her breeding program.

Since moving from Massachusetts to Pennsylvania in 1976, the Sabrina dogs have been shown quite sparingly. As Marcia Richardson says, "I'd rather have a live non-champion than a dead champion," and she greatly fears the dangers of parvo and the newer "B" virus, which is certainly understandable! Hopefully, however, before too long she will again be inclined to make a few more shows as the lovely youngsters she is breeding should have bright futures in the ring if given the opportunity.

Su-Le

Su-Le Maltese are really a "family affair," the kennel being named for Susan and Lisa Bergquist, daughters of owner Barbara (Mrs. R.C.) Bergquist of New Boston, Michigan.

Barbara Bergquist has been showing owner-handled Maltese since 1968, when she fell in love with the beautiful bitch Champion Aennchen's Poona Dancer and decided that she, too, must have a Maltese. Thus it was that her first Maltese bitch, Su-Le's Robin of Eng, joined the household, purchased from Anna Engstrom. As Barbara says, "I stepped into the Maltese ring with Robin and have been stepping ever since." Robin completed her title in short order when one year old and then went on to compete as a Special. She won a few Group firsts, lost a

Ch. Su-Le's Man-O-War Bird, a Wren son, 4 pound dog who finished at 11 months age. Bred, owned and handled by Mrs. R.C. (Barbara) Bergquist, New Boston, Michigan.

Ch. Su-Le's Jonina, by Ch. To The Victor of Eng ex Ch. Su-Le's Jacana, snapped informally with breeder Barbara Bergquist.

few, and took many placements. She is a small bitch, tipping the scales at four and a half pounds, and a sheer delight to show. She raised three champion offspring, including Champion Su-Le's Sandpiper, who was awarded the American Maltese Association's Maltese Merit Award as the sire of eight champions; and Champion Su-Le's Roadrunner, a three and a half pound Group-winning dog who became the sire of twelve champions (Group and Best in Show winners among them) to gain the American Maltese Association Maltese Merit Award. Robin, who at fifteen years of age is still the beloved family companion, truly introduced the Bergquists to a wonderful world of breeding and showing outstanding Maltese!

Then came Champion To The Victor of Eng, shortly after Robin, who was owner-handled to his title in but six ring appearances. He earned one reserve award from the Puppy Class, then five straight major awards from Open, completing his championship under the renowned breeder and judge Aennchen Antonelli. This phenomenal little dog, at thirteen years of age, weighs four and a half pounds and is truly a living legend as the sire of sixty-five American champions, nine Canadian champions, and champion offspring in other countries around the world. Additionally, Victor has set numerous records for the breed, including being a Top Producer in 1972, 1976, 1977, 1979, 1980, 1981, and 1982 according to the Irene Schlintz ratings. He is currently Number Seven among all American Top Producing *toy* sires. Victor has sired fourteen "complete champion" litters, and many of his progeny have gone on to win all-breed Bests in Show, Toy Groups, and Specialty Show awards. At age thirteen, he still is alert and producing.

Among Victor's progeny is Champion Su-Le's Blue Bird, who has twenty champions to his own credit and was a Top Producer in 1978, 1979, and 1980.

American and Bermudian Champion Su-Le's Wren is a full sister, one year younger, to Robin, and at seventeen months of

Ch. Su-Le's Egret is owned by Barbara Bergquist, New Boston, Michigan.

Barbara Bergquist's beloved Am. and Can. Ch. Su-Le's Robin of Eng, now 15 years old, was this highly successful fancier's first introduction to the Maltese breed.

Ch. Su-Le's Wren of Eng winning the Toy Group her first time out as a "special" at age 13 months under judge Joe Faigel. Barbara Bergquist, owner, Su-Le's Maltese, New Boston, Michigan.

age, after many Group wins, she was handled by Mrs. Bergquist to the kennel's first all-breed Best in Show—a real thrill for her owner-handler! This four-pound mite has also carried on in the family tradition, producing two champions out of three puppies.

Mrs. Bergquist considers of primary importance to any breeder the owning of a top quality producing bitch, and she is well pleased with her homebred Champion Su-Le's Jacona who has gained prestige in the Maltese world by consistently producing quality puppies who in their turn have gone on to gain records both in the show ring and as producers. Jacona was a Top Producing Bitch for 1975, 1976, and 1978. She holds the record for bitches with fifteen champions, among the most notable of them being the all-breed and Specialty Best in Show winner Champion Su-Le's Jonina and Top Producer Champion Su-Le's Blue Bird. More than one hundred champions have entered the Bergquists' lives since they first were "bitten by the dog show bug," but the very *special* ones will always be Robin, Victor, Wren, and Jacona.

Mrs. Bergquist breeds on a very limited scale and lives by the motto "we breed our show stock and show our breeding stock."

Frequently asked what "type" Maltese she prefers, Mrs. Bergquist's invariable reply is "to me there are only two types: show quality and pet quality. If they aren't quality enough to show, they aren't quality enough to breed, as 'like begets like'."

Of the last six annual American Maltese Association National Specialties in which Su-Le Maltese have competed, five times they have been winners.

All of the Su-Le Maltese are named for birds, Mrs. Bergquist having long been an admirer of the beauty of these tiny creatures, as she is of the Maltese. Speaking of names, an amusing anecdote is that the kennel was originally intended to be known as Su-Li, for SUsan and LIsa. But when Mrs. Bergquist placed a large stationery order for letterheads, envelopes, business cards, and so on, and they all came back printed Su-L*e*, it was decided to let the name remain as printed because Mrs. Bergquist is not one to pass up a bargain and the printer offered it to her for half price if she would accept the order despite the error.

Both Mr. and Mrs. Bergquist are longtime members of the American Maltese Association, he having served as President and being the current Treasurer and she as the Corresponding Secretary.

Villa Malta (Margaret Rozik)

Villa Malta Kennels, the oldest to have remained constantly active in the United States as breeders of Maltese, were founded in the 1930's by Dr. and Mrs. Vincenzo Calvaresi at New Bedford, Massachusetts. Quickly it became one of the most successful and dominant in this breed's history, the Calvaresis producing generation after generation of outstandingly show-worthy dogs. For more information on these early dogs, we refer you to our chapter on the history and development of the breed in the United States.

On July 23rd 1966, having decided to move to Florida on a business venture which precluded his continuing the kennel and necessitated his resignation as a judge (this new interest was a commercial one involving dogs), Dr. Calvaresi handed over the keys to his kennel and the ownership of the Villa Malta name and dogs to Mrs. Margaret Rozik, a longtime friend, a Maltese person herself, and a professional handler who had piloted the great Champion Talia of Villa Malta and other of the Calvaresi dogs to exciting show successes. Mrs. Rozik, who lives at Belle Vernon, Pennsylvania took forty-five of the best dogs from there to her own kennel in Pennsylvania, where they joined the thirty-five dogs already in residence there, with Mrs. Rozik continuing to breed pure Villa Malta stock and doing a bit of showing, too.

Margaret (or Marge to her friends) Rozik saw a champion Maltese for the first time on April 4th 1940; the Maltese was Champion Villa Malta's Vivia, by the great early producer Champion Cupid of Hale Farms ex Champion Hale Farms Hermanita. Being interested in large breeds at that time, she thought no more about it. Then in 1945, she saw Champion Issa of Villa Malta, and this time it started her wanting a Maltese of her own. Time went on, and it was not until 1951 that she finally succumbed to temptation and brought one home from Chicago. Her husband's immediate reaction was, "What's that? It looks like a mop." But in no time at all the entire family dearly loved the new pet.

Around that period, Marge started to show, on a small scale, for Dr. Calvaresi. He handled his own dogs in the East as a rule and, with Marge, they had some shown on the West Coast. She says, in reminiscing, "I had no idea of coat care, was scared to death, and my poor Duffy (her own pet) really got the treatment

The great Ch. Talia of Villa Malta, famous Best in Show Maltese of the early 1960s, handled here by Marge Rozik for breeder-owners Dr. and Mrs. Vincenzo Calvaresi, Bedford, Mass.

Am. and Can. Ch. Villa Malta's Kimba in Aug. 1975. Wendell Sammet, handler, photo courtesy of Dee Shepherd.

Three of the Villa Malta Maltese owned by Margaret M. Rozik, Belle Vernon, Pennsylvania.

as I tried out everything I heard of on him. Believe me, experience is the best teacher."

During this period, Marge was also doing some breeding for the Calvaresis. She always dreaded having "Doc" come to get the puppies, as tears inevitably followed them.

Eventually, Marge Rozik bought her own little bitch on whom she put a title. This was Champion Evina of Villa Malta. Since then she has continued on, finishing many champions and winning Toy Groups and Bests in Show. Her favorites of the great winners have included Champion Musi of Villa Malta, Champion Talia of Villa Malta, Champion Lacy of Villa Malta, and many more.

The Calvaresis remained in Florida until January of 1978, after which they moved to Portugal. Mrs. Calvaresi has passed away, but Dr. Calvaresi has re-married, living with his wife in a lovely small villa, but without dogs.

The Florida project, for which Dr. Calvaresi made the move there, was an interesting one. As I recall, it was his plan to open a canine zoo, with dogs of every breed represented, as a tourist attraction. I remember his tremendous enthusiasm for the plan when he told me about it prior to leaving this area, but after that I did not hear from him so I have no idea how it turned out.

Marge Rozik has truly kept Villa Malta on the map. Although her showing is limited, she has finished a considerable number of champions, and her plan is to continue doing so. It is interesting that her granddaughter, De Anna Rozik, now seventeen years old, owns some of the dogs and hopes to carry on with them and with Villa Malta after she finishes school.

Her association with Maltese and with Villa Malta has been an experience filled with happiness for Marge Rozik, and she expresses her appreciation to Dr. and Mrs. Calvaresi for thirty-two great years of loving and owning these little white "people." As she says, "Maltese are the greatest!"

BEST OF
WINNERS

WESTMINSTER
KENNEL CLUB

1983

ASHBEY

Chapter V
Standards of the Maltese

The "standard of the breed", to which one sees and hears such frequent reference whenever purebred dogs are written of or discussed, is the word picture of what is considered to be the ideal specimen of the breed in question. It outlines, in minute detail, each and every feature of that breed, both in physical characteristics and in temperament, accurately describing the dog from whisker to tail, creating a clear impression of what is to be considered correct or incorrect, the features comprising "breed type," and the probable temperament and behavior patterns of typical members of that breed.

The standard is the guide for breeders endeavoring to produce quality dogs and for fanciers wishing to learn what is considered beautiful in these dogs; and it is the tool with which judges evaluate and make their decisions in the ring. The dog it describes is the one which we seek and to which we compare in making our evaluations. It is the result of endless hours spent in dedicated work by knowledgeable members of each breed's parent Specialty Club, resulting from the combined efforts of the club itself, its individual members, and finally the American Kennel Club by whom official approval must be granted prior to each standard's acceptance, or that of any amendments or changes to it, in the United States. Breed standards are based on

Opposite page: Michael Wolf taking Best of Winners at Westminster 1983 with Ch. Gemmery's Alexandrite-Tee, by Ch. Gemmery's Turquoise Bean ex Ch. Gemmery's Coral Maker, bred by Naomi Erickson. Alex finished undefeated in 5 shows with two 5-point "majors." Co-owned by Mr. Wolf and David Fitzpatrick, Oxford, Pennsylvania.

intensive study of breed history, earlier standards in the United States or in the countries where these dogs originated or were recognized prior to introduction to the United States, and the purposes for which the breed was originally created and developed. All such factors have played their part in the drawing up of our present standards.

The American Standard

GENERAL APPEARANCE: The Maltese is a toy dog covered from head to foot with a mantle of long, silky, white hair. He is gentle-mannered and affectionate, eager and sprightly in action, and, despite his size, possessed of the vigor needed for the satisfactory companion.

HEAD: Of medium length and in proportion to the size of the dog. *The skull* is slightly rounded on top, the stop moderate. *The drop ears* are rather low set and heavily feathered with long hair that hangs close to the head. *Eyes* are set not too far apart; they are very dark and round, their black rims enhancing the gentle yet alert expression. *The muzzle* is of medium length, fine and tapered, but not snipy. *The nose* is black. *The teeth* meet in an even, edge-to-edge bite or in a scissors bite.

NECK: Sufficient length of neck is desirable as promoting a high carriage of the head.

BODY: Compact, the height from the withers to the ground equalling the length from the withers to the root of the tail. Shoulder blades are sloping, the elbows well knit and held close to the body. The back is level in topline, the ribs well sprung. The chest is fairly deep, the loins taut, strong, and just slightly tucked up underneath.

TAIL: A long-haired plume carried gracefully over the back, its tip lying to the side over the quarter.

LEGS AND FEET: Legs are fine-boned and nicely feathered. Forelegs are straight, their pastern joints well knit and devoid of appreciable bend. Hind legs are strong and moderately angulated at stifles and hocks. The feet are small and round, with toe pads black. Scraggly hairs on the feet may be trimmed to give a neater appearance.

COAT AND COLOR: The coat is single, that is, without undercoat. It hangs long, flat, and silky over the sides of the body almost, if not quite, to the ground. The long head-hair may be tied up in a topknot or it may be left hanging. Any suggestions of kinkiness, curliness, or woolly texture is objectionable. Color, pure white. Light tan or lemon on the ears is permissible, but not desirable.

SIZE: Weight under 7 pounds, with from 4 to 6 pounds preferred. Over-all quality is to be favored over size.

GAIT: The Maltese moves with a jaunty, smooth, flowing gait. Viewed from the side, he gives an impression of rapid movement, size considered. In the stride, the forelegs reach straight and free from the shoulders, with elbows close. Hind legs to move in a straight line. Cowhocks or any suggestion of hind leg toeing in or out are faults.

TEMPERAMENT: For all his diminutive size, the Maltese seems to be without fear. His trust and affectionate responsiveness are very appealing. He is among the gentlest mannered of all little dogs, yet he is lively and playful as well as vigorous.

Approved March 10th, 1964

Before 1964 an earlier standard was drawn up by the National Maltese Dog Club and was in use for several decades. Because of the historical value of this standard, we feel it should be included here.

GENERAL APPEARANCE: Intelligent, sprightly, affectionate with long straight coat hanging evenly down each side, the parting extending from nose to root of tail. Although the frame is hidden beneath a mantle of hair, the general appearance should suggest a vigorous, well-proportioned body.

WEIGHT: Not to exceed 7 pounds. Smaller the better. Under 3 pounds ideal.

COLOR: Pure white.

COAT: Long, straight, silky but strong and of even texture throughout. No undercoat.

HEAD: In proportion to size of the dog—should be of fair length: the *skull* slightly round, rather broad between the ears and moderately well defined at the temples, *i.e.* exhibiting a moderate amount of stop and not in one straight line from nose to occiput bone.

MUZZLE: Not lean nor snipey but delicately proportioned.

NOSE: Black.

EARS: Drop ears set slightly low, profusely covered with long hair.
EYES: Very dark—not too far apart—expression alert but gentle: black eye rims give a more beautiful expression.
LEGS: Short, straight, fine-boned and well feathered.
FEET: Small with long feathering.
BODY AND SHAPE: Back short and level. Body low to ground, deep loins.
TAIL AND CARRIAGE: Tail well feathered with long hair, gracefully carried, its end resting on the hind quarters and side.

SCALE OF POSITIVE POINTS

Weight and size	20
Coat	20
Color	10
Body and shape	10
Tail and its carriage	10
Head	5
Eyes	5
Ears	5
Legs	5
Feet	5
Nose	5
Total	100

SCALE OF NEGATIVE POINTS

Hair clipped from face or feet	20
Kinky, curly or outstanding coat	15
Uneven texture of coat	10
Yellow or any color on ears or coat	10
Undershot or overshot jaws	10
Prominent or bulging eyes	10
Pig nose or deep stop	10
Roach back	5
Legginess	5
Butterfly or Dudley nose	5
Total	100

Viceroy Kathan's Honeycomb with her breeder-handler Kathy DiGiacomo. Honeycomb is owned by Laura Ford.

It is especially interesting to note the areas in which the 1964 revision brought about changes and the difference in thinking they represent, for obvious changes in size evaluation and in color are very basic in this breed.

The present standard and the earlier one both place seven pounds as the top limit on weight. The current one gives four to six pounds as the preferred size and then adds that "Over-all quality is to be favored over size." The former standard, however, says "Smaller the better. Under 3 pounds ideal." The older standard also allots twenty points in favor of weight and size.

There are many diverse opinions at the present time on the subject of size, one school of thought being that as they are *toy* dogs, smaller than the extreme limit is better and that perhaps there is a tendency toward too large a size being accepted today. But, of course, as judges we have no choice other than to follow the words of the standard.

On the subject of color, "pure white" with ten negative points for any deviation from this was the feeling expressed in the earlier standard, while now "light tan or lemon on the ears is permissible but not desirable." This leniency undoubtedly was brought about by the deficiency in pigmentation (albinism) which may result from too steadfast a breeding program with pure white dogs, as has been the case in other breeds and some strains of dogs.

Interpretation of the American Standard

Learning the words of a breed standard is not all that difficult. Many people can recite them verbatim, with great confidence and few mistakes. The important thing, however, is that this not be a parrot-type procedure, or a case of knowing the words but not understanding what it is they are telling us. The ability to mechanically repeat what is written in a standard has little value unless one truly understands these words and possesses the ability to apply them to the dogs themselves. This is where people sometimes fall short, occasionally even including judges.

When a Maltese fancier has thoroughly acquainted himself with the standard's words, then it becomes important to cultivate the habit, every time one looks at a member of the breed, of mentally comparing this dog with those words. Some will adhere closely to them; others will not. The Maltese fancier, especially one planning to become a breeder or an exhibitor and perhaps eventually a judge, never should miss the opportunity of learning to use the familiarity with the standard's specifications which he has gained and working towards acquiring the art of applying them to each feature of every Maltese he sees. You'll be amazed at how quickly and how well you can thus teach yourself about your breed.

From the moment we have started noticing purebred dogs, we have learned that type is of utmost importance. But do we truly understand the word, and what "type" means in a Maltese? How about balance, without which no animal can be truly excellent, even though he may possess an outstanding individual feature, or several? Then there is "soundness," to which people usually refer when speaking of the manner in which a dog gaits.

Type is a composite of the features, as outlined in each breed standard, which make that breed unique and set it apart from all other breeds of dog. As applied to the Maltese, one of correct type is a small dog, compact in build with a firm, level topline and proud demeanor, moving along smoothly and jauntily, head carried high on a neck of good length enabling the dog to do so, the picture enhanced by proper tail carriage flat on the back and further enhanced by the correct coat, which is an imporatant characteristic. The coat of a Maltese is a *single* coat (*i.e.,* one without undercoat) falling long and flat over the sides of the dog from head to tail, of a straight and silky texture absolutely without any trace of woolliness, wave, or curl. A "fluffy" coat is entirely atypical in a Maltese, just as is one of coarse texture or any kinky tendencies. This applies right down to head featherings, tail, and so on. Pigmentation is important to the typical Maltese expression, with deep black nose leather, lips, and eyerims essential. A Maltese of correct character (or type) must never appear shy or timid. Self-confidence and a happy attitude are typical, as is a dog who steps out smartly, with good reach and drive for his size, as he moves. This demeanor on the part of these tiny dogs truly "brings down the house" from the audience at dog shows and has won the breed a host of admirers throughout the canine world.

Balance is proportion. A well-balanced dog has neither glaring faults nor an outstanding feature or two with little to back it up.

Ch. Caramaya's Jorgy Boy weighs in at 4 pounds. By Ch. Caramaya's Bo-jangles (Ch. Joanne-Chen's Maya Dancer - Bayhammond's Tainie Dancer) ex Maltes'a Joy (Ch. Su-Le's Blue Jay - Ch. Cashmere's Maranna Dancer), he belongs to Elaine Bobb, Bobb's Maltese, Chicago, Illinois. He is pictured winning under Mildred Heald en route to his championship at Cudahy in 1981.

BEST OF WINNERS

CUDAHY K. C.

AUG. 8, 1981

KARLEN PHOTO

132

He is a dog in which everything seems to fit together nicely, catching attention by the overall picture presented. In the case of the Maltese, a dog to be well balanced must be compact and low to the ground with a head of medium length and a neck long enough to carry it high. This head is balanced by a foreface just medium long in comparison to the skull. Length of back from withers (point of shoulder) to tail set (root of tail) should equal the height from withers to ground for the compact look.

"Soundness," or correct typical action, is displayed by a Maltese moving along smoothly, holding its topline level, reaching out well in the forelegs and flexing stifles and hocks powerfully behind. Speed is not the test of correct action and, in fact, in excessive cases can completely disguise whether or not the dog is moving *correctly*. The forelegs should reach out straight and true from strong, correctly angulated shoulders, elbows held close to the body, the toes pointing straight ahead. The hindlegs should move in a straight line (a Maltese never should "crab" or "sidewind" as he travels) driving along in accordance with their moderate angulation. Viewed from behind, the hocks should be equidistant from each other (never cow-hocked), and they should travel straight ahead, never toeing in or out. The action should appear smooth and fluid and effortless.

We feel that shoulders on the Maltese, as this is written during 1983, need to come under a bit of extra attention from the breeders as we have noticed some very beautiful dogs lacking in correctness here. A bad front often can be overlooked due to the length of coat disguising it, but topline and truly correct action cannot fail to suffer when that fault exists.

The current fad in the show ring is that of racing all dogs around the ring as though they were coursing hounds, and it is atypical and unbecoming in a great many cases. Don't you hate to see a tiny dog rushed along so fast that its feet barely touch the ground? I do, for under those circumstances it is impossible to evaluate whether or not the dog's conformation is equipping him to move in accordance with what is correct. All four feet of a moving dog should be able to touch the ground, and the speed should be adjusted accordingly.

There are no breed disqualifications in the Maltese standard; although, of course, those imposed by the American Kennel Club are effective in all breeds. These tell us that a dog who is

There is nothing prettier than a tiny Maltese stepping out! This one, handled by Dee Shepherd, at Santa Barbara in 1976.

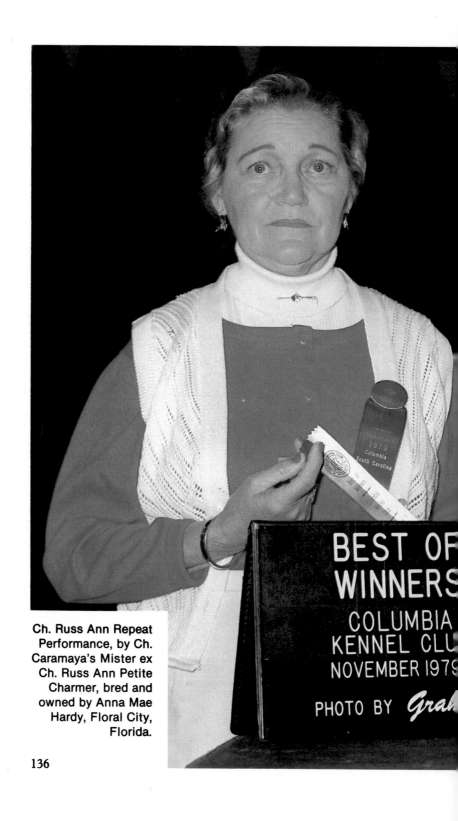

Ch. Russ Ann Repeat Performance, by Ch. Caramaya's Mister ex Ch. Russ Ann Petite Charmer, bred and owned by Anna Mae Hardy, Floral City, Florida.

Ch. March'en Lady Bug Dancer ex Sioux City Kennel Club Dog Show in 1976 with owner, Marcia Hostetter, Des Moines, Iowa.

blind, deaf, castrated, or spayed; a dog who has been changed in appearance by artificial means except as specified in its breed standard; or a male who does not have two normal testicles normally located in the scrotum may not compete at any A.K.C. dog show, except that a castrated male may be entered in the Stud Dog Class and a spayed bitch may be entered in the Brood Bitch Class where it is their progeny which will be judged. Any of the above conditions discovered by the judge lead to disqualifying action on his part.

The British Standard

CHARACTERISTICS: Sweet tempered and very intelligent.

GENERAL APPEARANCE: Should be smart, lively and alert. The action must be free, without extended weaving.

HEAD AND SKULL: From stop to centre of skull (centre between forepart of ears) and stop to tip of nose should be equally balanced. Stop should be defined. Nose should be pure black.

EYES: Should be dark brown, with black eyerims, set in centre cheeks and not bulging.

EARS: Should be long and well feathered and hanging close to the side of the head, the hair to be mingled with the coat at the shoulders.

MOUTH: Level or scissor bite with teeth even.

NECK: Of medium length—set on well sloped shoulders.

FOREQUARTERS: Legs should be short and straight. Shoulders well sloped.

BODY: Should be in every way well balanced and essentially short and cobby, with good rib spring and the back should be straight from the tip of the shoulders to the tail.

HINDQUARTERS: Legs should be short and nicely angulated.

FEET: Should be round and the pads of the feet should be black.

TAIL: Should be well arched over the back and feathered.

COAT: Should be good length, but not impeding action, of silky texture, not in any way woolly and should be straight. It should not be crimped and there should be no woolly undercoat.

COLOUR: Pure white, but slight lemon markings should not penalise.

SIZE: Not over 10 inches from ground to top of shoulder.

FAULTS: Bad mouth, over or undershot; gay tail; curly or woolly coat; brown nose; pink eye rims; unsound in any way.

NOTE: Male animals should have two apparently normal testicles fully descended into the scrotum.

The Australian Standard

The requirements of the Australian Standard for the Maltese are identical to those of the British Standard, except for a few minor differences in wording.

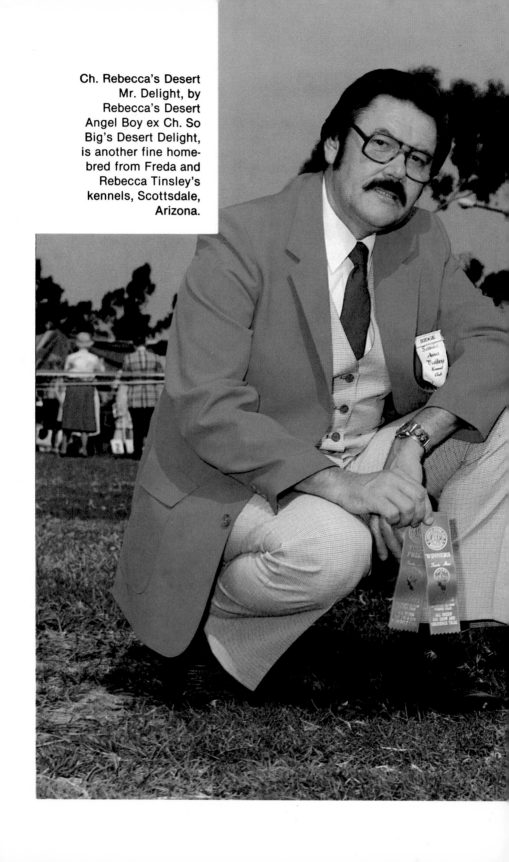

Ch. Rebecca's Desert Mr. Delight, by Rebecca's Desert Angel Boy ex Ch. So Big's Desert Delight, is another fine home-bred from Freda and Rebecca Tinsley's kennels, Scottsdale, Arizona.

Am., Can., Bda. Ch. Oak Ridge Country Charmer in his "Praising the Lord" pose. This picture was captured by photographer Diane Alverson as Charmer's owner, Carol Neth, entered the room.

Chapter VI
The Maltese Character

It would truly be difficult, if not entirely impossible, to find a more thoroughly delightful, charming, interesting, and satisfactory breed of dog to own as a companion than a Maltese. Their diminutive size makes them fit in well anywhere. Their intelligence and personality make them a pleasure to have around. And their beauty makes them a delight to the eye.

Although the Maltese is a tiny dog, every inch of it is filled with personality. The most commonly used adjective, we note, among writers speaking of this breed is "sparkling," which says it very well, as these little dogs do, indeed, seem to sparkle—not only in their gleaming white coats but also in their eagerness, alertness, and zest for life. A Maltese could never be called a dull companion. They are far too "on the button" for that. At the same time they are easy to manage due to their size and gentle personality. If you own a Maltese, it can be pure pleasure for you no matter what your interests. If you are a "stay-at-home" type, a Maltese is a super friend, loving to curl up in your lap as you read or watch television, to take walks with you, to play, or to just relax according to your mood.

If you are travel-minded, enjoying weekend trips or longer sojourns, your Maltese can accompany you with no problems. Small and lightweight enough to carry easily, either under arm or in a carrier made for the specific purpose, he is never a burden. And if you travel frequently by plane, he can fit very well, in his carrier, alongside you or under the seat. The Maltese also likes riding in cars and obviously is small enough usually to be welcome in motels and the homes of friends you may be visiting so long as he does not create any situation with pets belonging to your host who may resent canine guests, although the Maltese can do quite well at winning them over, too! It

Am., Can., Bda. Ch. Oak Ridge Country Charmer winning his first National Specialty under Mr. Frank Oberstar. Carol A. Neth, breeder-owner-handler.

would really be almost impossible to find man or beast who could dislike a Maltese!

Of course for apartment living, a small dog is far and away the easiest to manage. Your Maltese can, if it is more convenient for you, be trained to use a newspaper as his bathroom, releasing you from the obligation of having to take him out at periodic intervals. A paper-trained dog can be a blessing to people who are in business and away from home all day, especially if they live alone or if the other members of the family must also be absent. And obviously this would not be practical with other than a tiny breed such as the Maltese.

The Maltese fares equally well in the suburbs or the country. Of course, like any other dog, they need the protection of a fenced area if they are to enjoy the outdoors. Most definitely they should never be turned loose to fend for themselves as their courage far exceeds their size and strength, and they could thus become involved in situations they are not equipped to handle.

While you might not have thought so, the Maltese makes an alert and efficient watch dog, being quick to notice any strange "happenings" and to sound the alarm. The idea that a watch dog must be so huge as to terrorize an intruder due to his obvious size and power is not quite true. Probably being faced with such a dog does give pause to one who is bent on mischief, but it is not only a trained attack dog who can protect your possessions. The major fear of an intruder is having his presence called to attention by *noise*, and a furiously barking small dog (one too small for him to get hold of to silence and clever about dodging behind or under furniture should a move be made toward him under such circumstances) can be quite an effective tormentor! So never underrate the watch dog capabilities of the Maltese, which you should encourage by praising him for barking ferociously if someone he does not know comes to your door.

Maltese love children but do not always make the best pets for youngsters not yet old enough to understand the fact that these dogs are fine-boned, diminutive creatures who can be seriously hurt by rough handling or mauling. Thus if you have both a child and a Maltese, be very careful to teach the child that this is a fragile little animal no matter how courageous it may seem and that its delicate build and fine bones make essential the gentlest of care from a child. Young children should have a larger, more

rugged and sturdier breed than any of the Toys, actually, unless they are exceptionally aware and considerate of the harm they can do their pet by rough treatment.

The texture of the Maltese coat makes the dog an easy one to keep groomed, as the silky single coat does not mat so readily as the double-coated breeds with soft undercoat. Also these long, silky hairs are easily removed from clothes or furniture in case of shedding, which the Maltese does *not* seem to do as copiously as do some breeds.

Your Maltese should enjoy a long, healthful life if cared for sensibly. They are hardy and strong despite being so small, and they are not a delicate breed where health is concerned. Like any dog, attention should be paid to their shots, diet, and general care, with periodic checks by your veterinarian for worms and other possible problems. Other than this, which is a necessity no matter what breed or type of dog you choose, you will find your Maltese trouble-free and undemanding to own.

Ch. Jo Ann's Merrylane Matchmaker winning the Toy Group at Kennel Club of Yorkville, Illinois under Mrs. Ruth Turner in June 1982. Sired by Ch. Tumblemere's Beau Jester ex Ch. Debbie's Majestic Crysta Lyn; bred, owned and handled by Jo Ann Dinsmore, Arlington Heights, Illinois. This handsome little dog has won Best of Breed 75 times, Best Toy 8 times, and has 33 additional Group placements.

Opposite page: Ch. Su-Le's Mynah II is an excellent example of why so many people find the Maltese so endearing and beautiful a breed. Elyse R. Fischer, Port Washington, New York, and Kathy DiGiacomo, Fair Lawn, New Jersey, are the co-owners.

148

Don't you really *have* to have a Maltese puppy? This tiny charmer belongs to Gail Hennessey, Wappingers Falls, New York.

Chapter VII
The Purchase Of Your
Dog Or Puppy

Careful consideration should be given to what breed of dog you wish to own prior to your purchase of one. If several breeds are attractive to you, and you are undecided which you prefer, learn all you can about the characteristics of each before making your decision. As you do so, you are thus preparing yourself to make an intelligent choice; and this is very important when buying a dog who will be, with reasonable luck, a member of your household for at least a dozen years or more. Obviously since you are reading this book, you have decided on the breed—so now all that remains is to make a good choice.

It is never wise to just rush out and buy the first cute puppy who catches your eye. Whether you wish a dog to show, one with whom to compete in obedience, or one as a family dog purely for his (or her) companionship, the more time and thought you invest as you plan the purchase, the more likely you are to meet with complete satisfaction. The background and early care behind your pet will reflect in the dog's future health and temperament. Even if you are planning the purchase purely as a pet, with no thoughts of showing or breeding in the dog's or puppy's future, it is essential that if the dog is to enjoy a trouble-free future you assure yourself of a healthy, properly raised puppy or adult from sturdy, well-bred stock.

Throughout the pages of this book you will find the names and locations of many well-known and well-established kennels in various areas. Another source of information is the American Kennel Club (51 Madison Avenue, New York, New York 10010) from whom you can obtain a list of recognized breeders in the vicinity of your home. If you plan to have your dog campaigned by a professional handler, by all means let the handler help you locate and select a good dog. Through their numerous clients,

Ch. Rebecca's Pretty Girl, by Rebecca's Desert Mr. Lover ex Rebecca's Joy of So Big, finished quickly, then was cut down and as we go to press is waiting to be bred to Valentino, which will be excellent line-breeding as their sires are littermates from Rebecca Tinsley's Junior Showmanship Dog. Freda Tinsley, owner, Rebecca's Maltese, Scottsdale, Arizona.

handlers have access to a variety of interesting show prospects; and the usual arrangement is that the handler re-sells the dog to you for what his cost has been, with the agreement that the dog be campaigned for you by him throughout the dog's career. I most strongly recommend that prospective purchasers follow these suggestions, as you thus will be better able to locate and select a satisfactory puppy or dog.

Your first step in searching for your puppy is to make appointments at kennels specializing in the chosen breed, where you can visit and inspect the dogs, both those available for sale and the kennel's basic breeding stock. You are looking for an active, sturdy puppy with bright eyes and intelligent expression and who is friendly and alert; avoid puppies who are hyperactive, dull, or listless. The coat should be clean and thick, with no sign of parasites. The premises on which he was raised should look (and smell) clean and be tidy, making it obvious that the puppies and their surroundings are in capable hands. Should the kennels featuring the breed you intend owning be sparse in your area or not have what you consider attractive, do not hesitate to contact others at a distance and purchase from them if they seem better able to supply a puppy or dog who will please you *so long as it is a recognized breeding kennel of that breed*. Shipping dogs is a regular practice nowadays, with comparatively few problems when one considers the number of dogs shipped each year. A reputable, well-known breeder wants the customer to be satisfied; thus he will represent the puppy fairly. Should you not be pleased with the puppy upon arrival, a breeder such as I have described will almost certainly permit its return. A conscientious breeder takes real interest and concern in the welfare of the dogs he or she causes to be brought into the world. Such a breeder also is proud of a reputation for integrity. Thus on two counts, for the sake of the dog's future and the breeder's reputation, to such a person a *satisfied* customer takes precedence over a sale at any cost.

If your puppy is to be a pet or "family dog," I feel the earlier the age at which it joins your household the better. Puppies are weaned and ready to start out on their own, under the care of a sensible new owner, at about six weeks old; and if you take a young one, it is often easier to train it to the routine of your household and your requirements of it than is the case with an older dog which, even though still a puppy technically, may have

Ch. Oak Ridge Dust Buster about to become a champion from the puppy classes. Carol Neth handling.

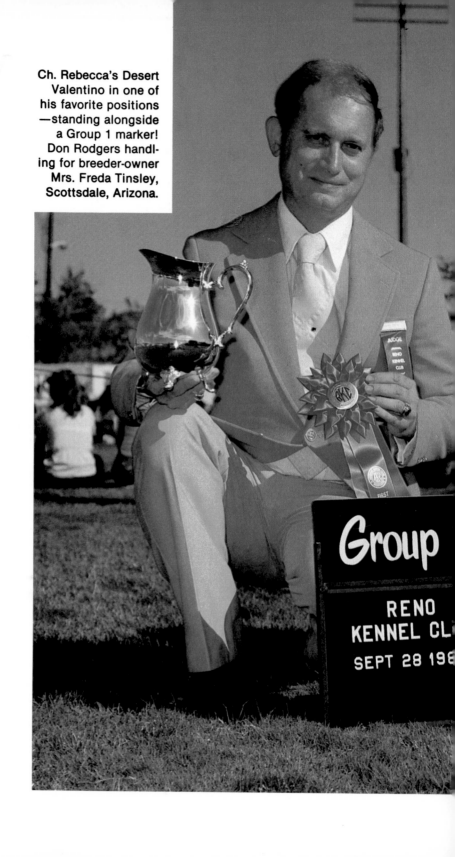

Ch. Rebecca's Desert Valentino in one of his favorite positions —standing alongside a Group 1 marker! Don Rodgers handling for breeder-owner Mrs. Freda Tinsley, Scottsdale, Arizona.

Group

RENO
KENNEL CL

SEPT 28 196

already started habits you will find difficult to change. The younger puppy is usually less costly, too, as it stands to reason the breeder will not have as much expense invested in it. Obviously, a puppy that has been raised to five or six months old represents more in care and cash expenditure on the breeder's part than one sold earlier and therefore should be and generally is priced accordingly.

There is an enormous amount of truth in the statement that "bargain" puppies seldom turn out to be that. A "cheap" puppy, cheaply raised purely for sale and profit, can and often does lead to great heartbreak including problems and veterinarian's bills which can add up to many times the initial cost of a properly reared dog. On the other hand, just because a puppy is expensive does not assure one that is healthy and well reared. I know of numerous cases where unscrupulous dealers have sold for several hundred dollars puppies that were sickly, in poor condition, and such poor specimens that the breed of which they were supposedly members was barely recognizable. So one cannot always judge a puppy by price alone. Common sense must guide a prospective purchaser, plus the selection of a *reliable*, well-recommended dealer whom you know to have well satisfied customers or, best of all, a specialized breeder. You will probably find the fairest pricing at the kennel of a breeder. Such a person, experienced with the breed in general and with his or her own stock in particular, through extensive association with these dogs has watched enough of them mature to have obviously learned to assess quite accurately each puppy's potential—something impossible where such background is non-existent.

One more word on the subject of pets. Bitches make a fine choice for this purpose as they are usually quieter and more gentle than the males, easier to house train, more affectionate, and less inclined to roam. If you do select a bitch and have no intention of breeding or showing her, by all means have her spayed, for your sake and for hers. The advantages to the owner of a spayed bitch include avoiding the nuisance of "in season" periods which normally occur twice yearly, with the accompanying eager canine swains haunting your premises in an effort to get close to your female, plus the unavoidable messiness and spotting of furniture and rugs at this time, which can be annoying if she is a household companion in the habit of sharing your

Could anyone *possibly* resist a Maltese puppy? This is Alex, who grew up to become Ch. Gemmery's Alexandrite-Tee. Owned by Michael Wolf and David Fitzpatrick, Christiana, Pennsylvania.

This is a baby photo of a future "star." Ch. Anna Marie's White Panther was purchased from the Stimmlers by Dr. Kenneth H. Knopf of Larchmont, New York and piloted to many important wins by Jane and Bob Forsyth.

A recently completed championship at Pegden Kennels, Sugar
Land, Texas, is that of Ch. Pegden's Luck of the Irish whose beauty
and splendid type are clearly evident here, caught by Denny
Mounce's camera. Co-owned by Peggy Lloyd and Denny Mounce.

Opposite page: Ch. Martin's Chanel-Cid, back
home a champion from handler Barbara Alderman. By Ch. Martin's Michael-Cid ex Michael's
Cookie. Breeder-owner-photographer, Marjorie
Martin, Martin's Maltese, Columbus, Ohio.

sofa or bed. As for the spayed bitch, she benefits as she grows older because this simple operation almost entirely eliminates the possibility of breast cancer ever occurring. I personally believe that all bitches should eventually be spayed—even those used for show or breeding when their careers are ended—in order that they may enjoy a happier, healthier old age. Please take note, however, that a bitch who has been spayed (or an altered dog) *cannot be shown at American Kennel Club Dog shows once this operation has been performed.* Be certain that you are *not*interested in showing her before taking this step.

Also in selecting a pet, never underestimate the advantages of an older dog, perhaps a retired show dog or a bitch no longer needed for breeding, who may be available quite reasonably priced by a breeder anxious to place such a dog in a loving home. These dogs are settled and can be a delight to own, as they make wonderful companions, especially in a household of adults where raising a puppy can sometimes be a trial.

Everything we have said about careful selection of your pet puppy and its place of purchase applies, but with many further considerations, when you plan to buy a show dog or foundation stock for a future breeding program. Now is the time for an in-depth study of the breed, starting with every word and every illustration in this book and all others you can find written on the subject. The standard of the breed now has become your guide, and you must learn not only the words but also how to interpret them and how they are applicable in actual dogs before you are ready to make an intelligent selection of a show dog.

If you are thinking in terms of a dog to show, obviously you must have learned about dog shows and must be in the habit of attending them. This is fine, but now your activity in this direction should be increased, with your attending every single dog show within a reasonable distance from your home. Much can be learned about a breed at ringside at these events. Talk with the breeders who are exhibiting. Study the dogs they are showing. Watch the judging with concentration, noting each decision made and attempt to follow the reasoning by which the judge has reached it. Note carefully the attributes of the dogs who win and, for your later use, the manner in which each is presented. Close your ears to the ringside know-it-alls, usually novice owners of only a dog or two and very new to the Fancy, who have only derogatory remarks to make about all that is taking place unless they happen to win. This is the type of exhibitor who "comes and goes" through the Fancy and whose interest is usually of very short duration owing to lack of knowledge and dissatisfaction caused by the failure to recognize the need to learn. You, as a fancier who we hope will last and enjoy our sport over many future years, should develop independent thinking at this stage; you should learn to draw your own conclusions about the merits, or lack of them, seen before you in the ring and thus, sharpen your own judgment in preparation for choosing wisely and well.

Note carefully which breeders campaign winning dogs, not just an occasional isolated good one but consistent, homebred winners. It is from one of these people that you should select your own future "star."

If you are located in an area where dog shows take place only occasionally or where there are long travel distances involved, you will need to find another testing ground for your ability to select a worthy show dog. Possibly, there are some representative kennels raising this breed within a reasonable distance. If so, by all means ask permission of the owners to visit the kennels and do so when permission is granted. You may not necessarily buy then and there, as they may not have available what you are seeking that very day, but you will be able to see the type of dog being raised there and to discuss the dogs with the breeder. Every time you do this, you add to your knowledge. Should one of these kennels have dogs which especially appeal to you, perhaps you could reserve a show-prospect puppy from a coming litter. This is frequently done, and it is often worth waiting for a puppy, unless you have seen a dog with which you are truly greatly impressed and which is immediately available.

We have already discussed the purchase of a pet puppy. Obviously this same approach applies in a far greater degree when the purchase involved is a future show dog. The only place at which to purchase a show prospect is from a breeder who raises show-type stock; otherwise, you are almost certainly doomed to disappointment as the puppy matures. Show and breeding kennels obviously cannot keep all of their fine young stock. An active breeder-exhibitor is, therefore, happy to place promising youngsters in the hands of people also interested in showing and winning with them, doing so at a fair price according to the

At thirteen months of age, Dot's Brewin Trouble from Dot's Yorkie Kennels, shown here with Katrina Helwig, was in the midst of a whirlwind career when the author awarded it Best of Winners in the mid-1970's at Santa Barbara.

Opposite page: Martin's Charmin' Charles at 2 weeks. By Ch. Noble Faith's Charmin' Fella ex Ch. Martin's Chanel-Cid. Breeder-owner-photographer, Marjorie Martin, Martin's Maltese, Columbus, Ohio.

quality and prospects of the dog involved. Here again, if no kennel in your immediate area has what you are seeking, do not hesitate to contact top breeders in other areas and to buy at long distance. Ask for pictures, pedigrees, and a complete description. Heed the breeder's advice and recommendations, after truthfully telling exactly what your expectations are for the dog you purchase. Do you want something with which to win just a few ribbons now and then? Do you want a dog who can complete his championship? Are you thinking of the real "big time" (*i.e.*, seriously campaigning with Best of Breed, Group wins, and possibly even Best in Show as your eventual goal)? Consider it all carefully in advance; then honestly discuss your plans with the breeder. You will be better satisfied with the results if you do this, as the breeder is then in the best position to help you choose the dog who is most likely to come through for you. A breeder selling a show dog is just as anxious as the buyer for the dog to succeed, and the breeder will represent the dog to you with truth and honesty. Also, this type of breeder does not lose interest the moment the sale has been made but when necessary will be right there ready to assist you with beneficial advice and suggestions based on years of experience.

As you make inquiries of at least several kennels, keep in mind that show-prospect puppies are less expensive than mature show dogs, the latter often costing close to four figures, and sometimes more. The reason for this is that, with a puppy, there is always an element of chance, the possibility of its developing unexpected faults as it matures or failing to develop the excellence and quality that earlier had seemed probable. There definitely is a risk factor in buying a show-prospect puppy. Sometimes all goes well, but occasionally the swan becomes an ugly duckling. Reflect on this as you consider available puppies and young adults. It just might be a good idea to go with a more mature, though more costly, dog if one you like is available.

When you buy a mature show dog, "what you see is what you get"; and it is not likely to change beyond coat and condition which are dependent on your care. Also advantageous for a novice owner is the fact that a mature dog of show quality almost certainly will have received show ring training and probably match show experience, which will make your earliest handling ventures far easier.

The look of a future winner. It was a 5-point "major" from the puppy class for soon-to-become Ch. Rebecca's Desert Sheik, with breeder-owner Mrs. Freda Tinsley, Scottsdale, Arizona.

Villa Norma's White Tornado and Ch. Villa Norma's Charisma make it a double victory at Eastern Dog Club for Wendell Sammet and Dee Shepherd.

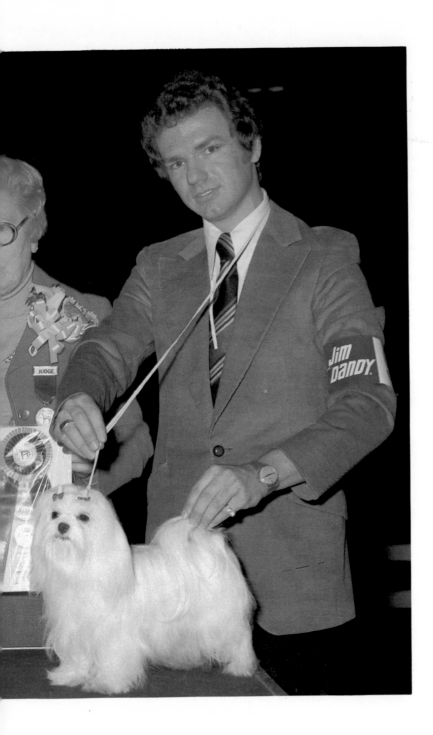

This exquisite Maltese is Viceroy Kathan's Honeycomb, who was bred by Kathy Di Giacomo and is owned by Laura Ford.

Frequently it is possible to purchase a beautiful dog who has completed championship but who, owing to similarity in bloodlines, is not needed for the breeder's future program. Here you have the opportunity of owning a champion, usually in the two- to five-year-old range, which you can enjoy campaigning as a "special" (for Best of Breed competition) and which will be a settled, handsome dog for you and your family to enjoy with pride.

If you are planning foundation for a future kennel, concentrate on acquiring one or two really superior bitches. These need not necessarily be top show-quality, but they should represent your breed's finest producing bloodlines from a strain noted for producing quality, generation after generation. A proven matron who is already the dam of show-type puppies is, of course, the ideal selection; but these are usually difficult to obtain, no one being anxious to part with so valuable an asset. You just might strike it lucky, though, in which case you are off to a flying start. If you cannot find such a matron available, select a young bitch of finest background from top producing lines who is herself of decent type, free of obvious faults, and of good quality.

Great attention should be paid to the pedigree of the bitch from whom you intend to breed. If not already known to you, try to see the sire and dam. It is generally agreed that someone starting with a breed should concentrate on a fine collection of top-flight bitches and raise a few litters from these before considering keeping one's own stud dog. The practice of buying a stud and then breeding everything you own or acquire to that dog does not always work out well. It is better to take advantage of the many noted sires who are available to be used at stud, who represent all of the leading strains, and in each case carefully to select the one who in type and pedigree seems most compatible to each of your bitches, at least for your first several litters.

To summarize, if you want a "family dog" as a companion, it is best to buy it young and raise it to the habits of your household. If you are buying a show dog, the more mature it is, the more certain you can be of its future beauty. If you are buying foundation stock for a kennel, then bitches are better, but they must be from the finest *producing* bloodlines.

When you buy a pure-bred dog that you are told is eligible for registration with the American Kennel Club, you are entitled to receive from the seller an application form which will enable you to register your dog. If the seller cannot give you the application form you should demand and receive an identification of your dog consisting of the name of the breed, the registered names and numbers of the sire and dam, the name of the breeder, and your dog's date of birth. If the litter of which your dog is a part is already recorded with the American Kennel Club, then the litter number is sufficient identification.

Do not be misled by promises of papers at some later date. Demand a registration application form or proper identification as described above. If neither is supplied, do not buy the dog. So warns the American Kennel Club, and this is especially important in the purchase of show or breeding stock.

Ch. March'en Kewpie Dancer, by Ch. March'en Top Hat Dancer ex Ch. March'en Lady Bug Dancer, bred, owned and handled by Marcia Hostetter, Des Moines, Iowa. Taking Best of Opposite Sex at Southeastern Iowa in 1983. Dorothy Nickles, judge.

Daisy, Andy and Twitter. Three lovely Maltese belonging to Gail Hennessey, Chelsea Kennels, Wappingers Falls, New York.

With all the elegance that gained her a host of admirers, Ch. Our Enterprising Bebe stands informally in June 1980 showing off her many outstanding qualities. Annette Lurton handled this famous bitch for Susan Grubb.

Ch. Martin's Chanel-Cid at 2 months. By Ch. Martin's Michael-Cid ex Michael's Cookie. Breeder-owner-photographer, Marjorie Martin, Columbus, Ohio.

Chapter VIII
The Care of Your Puppy

Preparing for Your Puppy's Arrival

The moment you decide to be the new owner of a puppy is not one second too soon to start planning for the puppy's arrival in your home. Both the new family member and you will find the transition period easier if your home is geared in advance for the arrival.

The first things to be prepared are a bed for the puppy and a place where you can pen him up for rest periods. I am a firm believer that every dog should have a crate of its own from the very beginning, so that he will come to know and love it as his special place where he is safe and happy. It is an ideal arrangement, for when you want him to be free, the crate stays open. At other times you can securely latch it and know that the pup is safely out of mischief. If you travel with him, his crate comes along in the car; and, of course, in travelling by plane there is no alternative but to have a carrier for the dog. If you show your dog, you will want him upon occasion to be in a crate a good deal of the day. So from every consideration, a crate is a very sensible and sound investment in your puppy's future safety and happiness and for your own peace of mind.

The crates I recommend are the wooden ones with removable side panels, which are ideal for cold weather (with the panels in place to keep out drafts) and in hot weather (with the panels removed to allow better air circulation). Wire crates are all right in the summer, but they give no protection from cold or drafts. I intensely dislike aluminum crates due to the manner in which aluminum reflects surrounding temperatures. If it is cold, so is the metal of the crate; if it is hot, the crate becomes burning hot. For this reason I consider aluminum crates neither comfortable nor safe.

Su-Le's Atlantic Brent, owner-handled by Kathy DiGiacomo, Fair Lawn, New Jersey.

When you choose the puppy's crate, be certain that it is roomy enough not to become outgrown. The crate should have sufficient height so the dog can stand up in it as a mature dog and sufficient area so that he can stretch out full length when relaxed. When the puppy is young, first give him shredded newspaper as a bed; the papers can be replaced with a mat or turkish towels when the dog is older. Carpet remnants are great for the bottom of the crate, as they are inexpensive and in case of accidents can be quite easily replaced. As the dog matures and is past the chewing age, a pillow or blanket in the crate is an appreciated comfort.

Sharing importance with the crate is a safe area in which the puppy can exercise and play. If you are an apartment dweller, a baby's playpen for a toy dog or a young puppy works out well; for a larger breed or older puppy use a portable exercise pen

A Pegden Maltese at approximately three months age. Peggy Lloyd and Denny Mounce, owners, Sugar Land, Texas.

Ch. Bar None Buckineer at home. Michele Perlmutter, owner, Bar None Maltese, Ghent, New York.

which you can then use later when travelling with your dog or for dog shows. If you have a yard, an area where he can be outside in safety should be fenced in prior to the dog's arrival at your home. This area does not need to be huge, but it does need to be made safe and secure. If you are in a suburban area where there are close neighbors, stockade fencing works out best as then the neighbors are less aware of the dog and the dog cannot see and bark at everything passing by. If you are out in the country where no problems with neighbors are likely to occur, then regular chain-link fencing is fine. For added precaution in both cases, use a row of concrete blocks or railroad ties inside against the entire bottom of the fence; this precludes or at least considerably lessens the chances of your dog digging his way out.

Be advised that if yours is a single dog, it is very unlikely that it will get sufficient exercise just sitting in the fenced area, which is what most of them do when they are there alone. Two or more dogs will play and move themselves around, but from my own experience, one by itself does little more than make a leisurely tour once around the area to check things over and then lie down. You must include a daily walk or two in your plans if your puppy is to be rugged and well. Exercise is extremely important to a puppy's muscular development and to keep a mature dog fit and trim. So make sure that those exercise periods, or walks, a game of ball, and other such activities, are part of your daily program as a dog owner.

Ch. Su-Le's Jonina winning Best of Breed at the American Maltese Association National Specialty at Houston, Texas, in 1978, Annette Lurton handling.

Opposite page: Ch. Viceroy's Precious Moment, co-owned by Marlene Greenberg and Kathy DiGiacomo, handled by Terence Childs.

180

WINNERS
RIVERHEAD
NEL CLUB INC
APRIL 1983

If your fenced area has an outside gate, provide a padlock and key and a strong fastening for it, and use them, so that the gate can not be opened by others and the dog taken or turned free. The ultimate convenience in this regard is, of course, a door (unused for other purposes) from the house around which the fenced area can be enclosed, so that all you have to do is open the door and out into his area he goes. This arrangement is safest of all, as then you need not be using a gate, and it is easier in bad weather since then you can send the dog out without taking him and becoming soaked yourself at the same time. This is not always possible to manage, but if your house is arranged so that you could do it this way, I am sure you would never regret it due to the convenience and added safety thus provided. Fencing in the entire yard, with gates to be opened and closed whenever a caller, deliveryman, postman, or some other person comes on your property, really is not safe at all because people not used to gates and their importance are frequently careless about closing and latching gates *securely*. I know of many heartbreaking incidents brought about by someone carelessly only half closing a gate which the owner had thought to be firmly latched and the dog wandering out. For greatest security a fenced *area* definitely takes precedence over a fenced *yard*.

The puppy will need a collar (one that fits now, not one to be grown into) and lead from the moment you bring him home. Both should be an appropriate weight and type for his size. Also needed are a feeding dish and a water dish, both made preferably of unbreakable material. Your pet supply shop should have an interesting assortment of these and other accessories from which you can choose. Then you will need grooming tools of the type the breeder recommends and some toys. One of the best toys is a beef bone, either rib, leg, or knuckle (the latter the type you can purchase to make soup), cut to an appropriate size for your puppy dog. These are absolutely safe and are great exercise for the teething period, helping to get the baby teeth quickly out of the way with no problems. Equally satisfactory is Nylabone®, a nylon bone that does not chip or splinter and that "frizzles" as the puppy chews, providing healthful gum massage. Rawhide chews are safe, too, *IF made in the United States*. There was a problem a few years back owing to the chemicals with which some foreign rawhide toys had been treated, since which time we

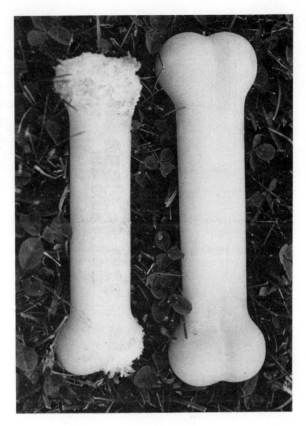

Do not discard a moderately chewed-up Nylabone (left). The frazzled ends act like a brush during chewing, cleaning the teeth and stimulating the gums of your Maltese.

have carefully avoided giving them to our own dogs. Also avoid plastics and any sort of rubber toys, *particularly* those with squeakers which the puppy may remove and swallow. If you want a ball for the puppy to use when playing with him, select one of very hard construction made for this purpose and do not leave it alone with him because he may chew off and swallow bits of the rubber. Take the ball with you when the game is over. This also applies to some of those "tug of war" type rubber toys which are fun when used with the two of you for that purpose but again should *not* be left behind for the dog to work on with his teeth. Bits of swallowed rubber, squeakers, and other such foreign articles can wreak great havoc in the intestinal tract—do all you can to guard against them.

Ch. Nicholas of Al-Mar in Japan with owner-handler Kohki Iijma.

Opposite page: Ch. Oak Ridge Pufnstuf, one of
the Oak Ridge top producers, owned by Carol A.
and Tom Neth, McMurray, Pennsylvania.

Roath's Merri of Merriville is dam of all the youngsters from Elaine Bobb's kennels sired by Ch. Caramaya's Jorgy Boy. A very excellent producing bitch, she was bred by Linda Ernst but now belongs to Elaine Bobb.

Too many changes all at once can be difficult for a puppy. For at least the first few days he is with you, keep him on the food and feeding schedule to which he is accustomed. Find out ahead of time from the breeder what he feeds his puppies, how frequently, and at what times of the day. Also find out what, if any, food supplements the breeder has been using and recommends. Then be prepared by getting in a supply of the same food so that you will have it there when you bring the puppy home. Once the puppy is accustomed to his new surroundings, then you can switch the type of food and schedule to fit your convenience, but for the first several days do it as the puppy expects.

Your selection of a veterinarian also should be attended to before the puppy comes home, because you should stop at the vet's office for the puppy to be checked over as soon as you leave the breeder's premises. If the breeder is from your area, ask him for recommendations. Ask your dog-owning friends for their opinions of the local veterinarians, and see what their experiences with those available have been. Choose someone whom several of your friends recommend highly, then contact him about your puppy, perhaps making an appointment to stop in at his office. If the premises are clean, modern, and well equipped, and if you like the veterinarian, make an appointment to bring the puppy in on the day of purchase. Be sure to obtain the puppy's health record from the breeder, including information on such things as shots and worming that the puppy has had.

Joining the Family

Remember that, exciting and happy an occasion as it is for you, the puppy's move from his place of birth to your home can be, for him, a traumatic experience. His mother and littermates will be missed. He quite likely will be awed or frightened by the change of surroundings. The person on whom he depended will be gone. Everything should be planned to make his arrival at your home pleasant—to give him confidence and to help him realize that yours is a pretty nice place to be after all.

Never bring a puppy home on a holiday. There just is too much going on with people and gifts and excitement. If he is in honor of an "occasion," work it out so that his arrival will be a few days earlier or, perhaps even better, a few days later than the "occasion." Then your home will be back to its normal routine and the puppy can enjoy your undivided attention. Try not to bring the puppy home in the evening. Early morning is the ideal time, as then he has the opportunity of getting acquainted and the initial strangeness should wear off before bedtime. You will find it a more peaceful night that way, I am sure. Allow the puppy to investigate as he likes, under your watchful eye. If you already have a pet in the household, keep a careful watch that the relationship between the two gets off to a friendly start or you may quickly find yourself with a lasting problem. Much of the future attitude of each toward the other will depend on what takes place that first day, so keep your mind on what they are doing and let your other activities slide for the moment. Be careful not to let your older pet become jealous by paying more attention to the puppy than to him, as that will start a bad situation immediately.

If you have a child, here again it is important that the relationship start out well. Before the puppy is brought home, you should have a talk with the youngster about puppies, so that it will be clearly understood that puppies are fragile and can easily be injured; therefore, they should not be teased, hurt, mauled, or overly rough-housed. A puppy is not an inanimate toy; it is a living thing with a right to be loved and handled respectfully, treatment which will reflect in the dog's attitude toward your child as both mature together. Never permit your children's playmates to mishandle the puppy, as I have seen happen, tormenting the puppy until it turns on the children in self-defense. Children

Ch. Joanne-Chen's Mino Maya Dancer winning Best in Show at Council Bluffs in 1980. Daryl Martin handling for Blanche Tenerowicz, Easthampton, Mass.

Opposite page: Another exquisite Missy Yuhl shot of the great Ch. Rebecca's Desert Valentino, Freda Tinsley, owner, Scottsdale, Arizona.

often do not realize how rough is too rough. You, as a responsible adult, are obligated to assure that your puppy's relationship with children is a pleasant one.

Do not start out by spoiling your puppy. A puppy is usually pretty smart and can be quite demanding. What you had considered to be "just for tonight" may be accepted by the puppy as "for keeps." Be firm with him, strike a routine, and stick to it. The puppy will learn more quickly this way, and everyone will be happier at the result. A radio playing softly or a dim night light are often comforting to a puppy as it gets accustomed to new surroundings and should be provided in preference to bringing the puppy to bed with you—unless, of course, you intend him to share the bed as a permanent arrangement

Socializing and Training Your New Puppy

Socialization and training of your puppy should start the very day of his arrival in your home. Never address him without calling him by name. A short, simple name is the easiest to teach as it catches the dog's attention quickly, so avoid elaborate call names. Always address the dog by the same name, not a whole series of pet names; the latter will only confuse the puppy.

Using his name clearly, call the puppy over to you when you see him awake and wandering about. When he comes, make a big fuss over him for being such a good dog. He thus will quickly associate the sound of his name with coming to you and a pleasant happening.

Several hours after the puppy's arrival is not too soon to start accustoming him to the feel of a light collar. He may hardly notice it; or he may struggle, roll over, and try to rub it off his neck with his paws. Divert his attention when this occurs by offering a tasty snack or a toy (starting a game with him) or by petting him. Before long he will have accepted the strange feeling around his neck and no longer appear aware of it. Next comes the lead. Attach it and then immediately take the puppy outside or otherwise try to divert his attention with things to see and sniff. He may struggle against the lead at first, biting at it and trying to free himself. Do not pull him with it at this point; just hold the end loosely and try to follow him if he starts off in any direction.

Normally his attention will soon turn to investigating his surroundings if he is outside or you have taken him into an unfamiliar room in your house; curiosity will take over and he will become interested in sniffing around the surroundings. Just follow him with the lead slackly held until he seems to have completely forgotten about it; then try with gentle urging to get him to follow you. Don't be rough or jerk at him; just tug gently on the lead in short quick motions (steady pulling can become a battle of wills), repeating his name or trying to get him to follow your hand which is holding a bite of food or an interesting toy. If you have an older lead-trained dog, then it should be a cinch to get the puppy to follow along after *him*. In any event, the average puppy learns quite quickly and will soon be trotting along nicely on the lead. Once that point has been reached, the next step is to teach him to follow on your left side, or heel. Of course this will not likely be accomplished all in one day but should be done with short training periods over the course of several days until you are satisfied with the result.

During the course of house training your puppy, you will need to take him out frequently and at regular intervals: first thing in the morning directly from the crate, immediately after meals, after the puppy has been napping, or when you notice that the puppy is looking for a spot. Choose more or less the same place to take the puppy each time so that a pattern will be established. If he does not go immediately, do not return him to the house as he will probably relieve himself the moment he is inside. Stay out with him until he has finished; then be lavish with your praise for his good behavior. If you catch the puppy having an accident indoors, grab him firmly and rush him outside, sharply saying "No!" as you pick him up. If you do not see the accident occur, there is little point in doing anything except cleaning it up, as once it has happened and been forgotten, the puppy will most likely not even realize why you are scolding him.

With a small breed, especially if you live in a big city or are away many hours at a time, having a dog that is trained to go on paper has some very definite advantages. To do this, one proceeds pretty much the same way as taking the puppy outdoors, except now you place the puppy on the newspaper at the proper time. The paper should always be kept in the same spot. An easy way to paper train a puppy if you have a playpen for it or an exer-

A lovely portrait by Gilbert of the famous Maltese Ch. Anna Marie's White Panther, owned by Dr. Kenneth H. Knopf, Larchmont, New York.

Opposite page: Pegden's Comin' Up Roses shows all the charm of an adorable 6-month-old Maltese baby. Owned by Peggy Lloyd and Denny Mounce, Pegden Kennels, Sugarland, Texas. Photo by Denny Mounce.

cise pen is to line the area with newspapers; then gradually, every day or so, remove a section of newspaper until you are down to just one or two. The puppy acquires the habit of using the paper; and as the prepared area grows smaller, in the majority of cases the dog will continue to use whatever paper is still available. My own experience, especially with Toy dogs, is that this works out well. It is pleasant, if the dog is alone for an excessive length of time, to be able to feel that if he needs it the paper is there and will be used.

The puppy should form the habit of spending a certain amount of time in his crate, even when you are home. Sometimes the puppy will do this voluntarily, but if not it should be taught to do so, which is accomplished by leading the puppy over by his collar, gently pushing him inside, and saying firmly "Down" or "Stay." Whatever expression you use to give a command, stick to the very same one each time for each act. Repetition is the big thing in training—and so is association with what the dog is expected to do. When you mean "Sit" always say exactly that. "Stay" should mean *only* that the dog should remain where he receives the command. "Down" means something else again. Do not confuse the dog by shuffling the commands, as this will create training problems for you.

As soon as he has had his immunization shots, take your puppy with you whenever and wherever possible. There is nothing that will build a self-confident, stable dog like socialization, and it is extremely important that you plan and give the time and energy necessary for this whether your dog is to be a show dog or a pleasant, well-adjusted family member. Take your puppy in the car so that he will learn to enjoy riding and not become carsick as dogs may do if they are infrequent travelers. Take him anywhere you are going where you are certain he will be welcome: visiting friends and relatives (if they do not have housepets who may resent the visit), busy shopping centers (keeping him always on lead), or just walking around the streets of your town. If someone admires him (as always seems to happen when we are out with puppies), encourage the stranger to pet and talk with him. Socialization of this type brings out the best in your puppy and helps him to grow up with a friendly outlook, liking the world and its inhabitants. The worst thing that can be done to a puppy's personality is to overly shelter him. By keeping him

The great stud dog, Ch. To The Victor of Eng, at 10 years of age. Barbara Bergquist, owner, New Boston, Michigan.

always at home away from things and people unfamiliar to him you may be creating a personality problem for the mature dog that will be a cross for you to bear later on.

Feeding Your Dog

Time was when providing nourishing food for our dogs involved a far more complicated procedure than people now feel is necessary. The old school of thought was that the daily ration must consist of fresh beef, vegetables, cereal, egg yolks, and cottage cheese as basics with such additions as brewer's yeast and vitamin tablets on a daily basis.

During recent years, however, many minds have changed regarding this procedure. We still give eggs, cottage cheese, and supplements to the diet, but the basic method of feeding dogs has changed; and the change has been, in the opinion of many authorities, definitely for the better. The school of thought now is that you are doing your dogs a favor when you feed them some of the fine commercially prepared dog foods in preference to your own home-cooked concoctions.

The reason behind this new outlook is easily understandable. The dog food industry has grown to be a major one, participated

Krystal's Pistachio 'n' Cream is typical of the lovely puppies being raised by Kris Collins at Krystal Maltese, Glendale Heights, Illinois.

in by some of the best known and most respected names in the American way of life. These trusted firms, it is agreed, turn out excellent products, so people are feeding their dog food preparations with confidence and the dogs are thriving, living longer, happier, and healthier lives than ever before. What more could we want?

There are at least half a dozen absolutely top-grade dry foods to be mixed with broth or water and served to your dog according to directions. There are all sorts of canned meats, and there are several kinds of "convenience foods," those in a packet which you open and dump out into the dog's dish. It is just that simple. The "convenience" foods are neat and easy to use when you are away from home, but generally speaking we prefer a dry food mixed with hot water or soup and meat. We also feel that the canned meat, with its added fortifiers, is more beneficial to the dogs than the fresh meat. However, the two can be alternated or, if you prefer and your dog does well on it, by all means use fresh ground beef. A dog enjoys changes in the meat part of his diet, which is easy with the canned food since all sorts of beef are available (chunk, ground, stewed, and so on), plus lamb, chicken, and even such concoctions as liver and egg, just plain liver flavor, and a blend of five meats.

There also is prepared food geared to every age bracket of your dog's life, from puppyhood on through old age, with special ad-

196

ditions or modifications to make it particularly nourishing and beneficial. Our grandparents, and even our parents, never had it so good where the canine dinner is concerned, because these commercially prepared foods are tasty and geared to meeting the dog's gastronomic approval.

Additionally, contents and nutrients are clearly listed on the labels, as are careful instructions for feeding just the right amount for the size, weight, and age of each dog.

With these foods we do not feel the addition of extra vitamins is necessary, but if you do there are several kinds of those, too, that serve as taste treats as well as being beneficial. Your pet supplier has a full array of them.

Of course there is no reason not to cook up something for your dog if you would feel happier doing so. But it seems to us unnecessary when such truly satisfactory rations are available with so much less trouble and expense.

How often you feed your dog is a matter of how it works out best for you. Many owners prefer to do it once a day. I personally think that two meals, each of smaller quantity, are better for the digestion and more satisfying to the dog, particularly if yours is a household member who stands around and watches preparations for the family meals. Do not overfeed. That is the shortest route to all sorts of problems. Follow directions and note carefully how your dog is looking. If your dog is overweight, cut back the quantity of food a bit. If the dog looks thin, then increase the amount. Each dog is an individual and the food intake should be adjusted to his requirements to keep him feeling and looking trim and in top condition.

From the time puppies are fully weaned until they are about twelve weeks old, they should be fed four times daily. From three months to six months of age, three meals should suffice. At six months of age the puppies can be fed two meals, and the twice daily feedings can be continued until the puppies are close to one year old, at which time feeding can be changed to once daily if desired.

If you do feed just once a day, do so by early afternoon at the latest and give the dog a snack, or biscuit or two, at bedtime.

Remember that plenty of fresh water should always be available to your puppy or dog for drinking. This is of utmost importance to his health.

Now that she is retired from the show ring, Ch. Martin's Chanel-Cid is sporting her new haircut, very suitable for the informality of home life. Marjorie Martin, breeder/owner/photographer, Martin's Maltese, Columbus, Ohio.

Chapter IX
Coat Care and Grooming
of Your Maltese

Grooming is of particular concern to every owner of a Maltese, for truly this little dog's coat *is* his crowning glory, and it is of utmost importance—whether you plan to show yours or just to enjoy his beauty at home—that it be kept in good condition and always at its best. The Maltese coat is not a difficult one to tend. If one avoids neglect, and follows a regular program of grooming, few if any problems should arise; and the rewards are worthwhile in the pleasure of keeping your dog at his sparkling best, arousing admiration from all who see him.

For this chapter on coat care and grooming, I have sought the advice of a noted breeder-owner-handler, whose dogs include a famed Best in Show winner, Champion Russ Ann Petite Charmer. This is Anna Mae Hardy, a lady who states, "Grooming and conditioning the Maltese is a fine art. There is nothing that bothers me more than to see a Maltese put in the ring dirty or hair all astray"—an opinion with which I am sure all of our readers agree. Mrs. Hardy learned to groom her dogs, condition them, and put up topknots during her early days of owning the breed. She has helped other owners maintain the coats of their dogs, sometimes even doing so through the mail if distance necessitated, and she has prepared a most useful grooming chart outline which she furnishes to all purchasers of her puppies. Having seen her grooming instructions, and the chart, and feeling that they make the subject easily understandable, we have sought and received Mrs. Hardy's permission to include them. (The instructions and chart appear toward the end of this chapter). We feel that our readers will find them useful and accurate guide to a well-groomed, properly coated Maltese.

To begin with, you will need equipment. This should include a grooming table (rubber-topped) especially made for this purpose. This is a great convenience when one has a dog (or dogs) of a "coated" breed, as its rubber top gives the dog a sense of security by preventing slipping and its folding legs permit its being easily stored when not in use. These are handy both at home for the regular grooming sessions and to be taken with you to shows to be used during last-minute preparations before taking your dog into the ring. A soft turkish towel or bath mat should be placed on the table; and the dog should be taught, from the beginning, to sit, stand, and lie on either side or flat on his stomach with his head down.

You will also need an electric hair dryer with blower for after bathing your dog.

Your grooming essentials should include a small or medium size pin brush, a large metal comb and a very small metal comb (the latter for topknots and the face beneath the eyes, a soft toothbrush for use on the face, long tweezers (for removing hair from within the ears), nail clippers, tapered scissors, small manicure type scissors for the feet, a fine knitting needle for parting the hair, small orthodontic rubber bands (sizes 3/8 inch and 3/16 inch), bows for the topknot, a good ear powder, protein shampoo and protein cream rinse (both of these preparations made for humans), a "bright white" shampoo especially made for white dogs, cornstarch, cotton swabs, and, if you are working on the coat of a future show dog, a cream conditioner not to be used until the puppy is nine to ten months old.

Your Maltese should be brushed at least every second day, which involves only a brief amount of time for so tiny a dog, to avoid formation of mats. Brush the coat with your small (or medium) pin brush, starting with the underpart of the dog, paying particular attention to the armpits and between the hindlegs as these are prime locations for mat formation. Should you find a mat (and most times one does), use your fingers to gently separate the hairs, pulling them loose from the mat a few at a time. *Never* try to brush or comb them through; this will cause pain to the dog and a loss of hair. Always "layer brush" as you work on your Maltese, taking a small section at a time, being certain to work right from the skin to the tips of the hair. Never rip at the coat with your brush as you will pull out hair in doing so.

Ch. Nicholas of Al-Mar, all combed out ready for the ring. Handled by Dee Shepherd, bred by Marjorie Lewis.

Do not brush superficially, just gliding over the top, as this will *not* bring about the desired results. Brushing should be a thorough, gentle process, missing not a single hair on the dog as you proceed.

Once the stomach, chest (from underneath the chin), and areas between and under the legs have been thoroughly brushed out, start work on the sides of the dog, layer brushing from the skin out.

At least once a week, and always after bathing, check the insides of your Maltese's ears, doing so gently with a cotton swab. Insert a bit of ear powder; then use your long tweezers to pull out any hair growing within the ear. This does not hurt and is a "must," for to leave the hair in the ear is an invitation to ear mites and ear infections which sometimes can lead to serious problems. Should evidence of either of these conditions occur, take your dog immediately to the veterinarian.

Keep the nails cut short with a nail clipper, removing only the tips growing beyond the pink "quick." It is important to keep after this, for if one does not, the "quicks" tend to overgrow along with the tips, making the nails bleed when shortened. Should this happen, or if you accidentally clip one too short, there is a preparation available at your pet supplier's which, when applied to the nail, will stop the bleeding almost instantly. But if you watch the nails carefully and keep them comfortably short, this should not happen.

The feet should be kept neat by trimming the hair from between the toes with your small, sharp manicure-type scissors, doing so with utmost care. The removal of this hair will give the dog better traction when walking. The outside edges of the feet should be trimmed in a half-moon, to accentuate the desired "small and round" appearance. Comb the feet before and after scissoring to avoid leaving "stragglers."

The hair around the rectum should be carefully trimmed for the sake of convenience and cleanliness, but please do not overdo this by taking away an excessive amount of hair as the dog will then look too "cleared away" to be attractive. Should your Maltese soil his skirts when relieving himself, see that it is removed promptly with a wad of tissue or a damp paper towel or by separating the hairs with your fingers so that it will fall off. Then if necessary stick his rear under a faucet to completely rinse away all traces; otherwise a stain or a sore rear (the latter sometimes necessitating a trip to the vet) may be the result.

In males, you should also clip the hair from around the penis, but *do not shorten* the length of hair down from the penis as it helps the urine to travel downward.

Every effort should be made to avoid stain on the face of a Maltese. Keep the hair under the eyes dry. It will stain a little when the puppy or dog is playing, after which a soft toothbrush with warm water should be used to wash it away, followed by drying with a soft cloth or towel and application of cornstarch. The latter should be worked back and forth into the hair with your fingers. Daily use of cornstarch is recommended.

The Maltese coat is not an oily one; therefore, too frequent bathings are not recommended as they will tend to dry out the natural oils. At the most, every ten days should be sufficient, depending on how the dog looks. House pets do tend to pick up

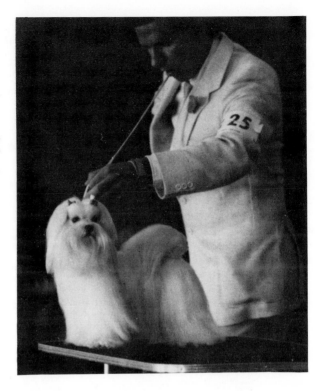

Ch. Bar None Sally May at the National Specialty, perfectly groomed and standing at attention. Michele Perlmutter, owner, Bar None Maltese, Ghent, New York.

more dirt from carpets and being outdoors, so when you find the brush starting to pull as it goes through the coat, it should be taken as a signal that a bath is in order.

Start bath preparations with a drop of castor oil in each eye and a wad of cotton in the ears to guard against soap or water entering either. Wet the dog thoroughly with a shampoo spray, using comfortably warm water; then shampoo. *Do not massage,* as this will mat the coat. Preferably squeeze and work the shampoo through the hair. If the dog is very dirty, shampoo a second time. Rinse very well, making certain that all traces of the shampoo are removed. Traces not removed can cause itching, leading to scratching and mats. Clean the whiskers with the toothbrush. Work a cream rinse through the coat, and then again rinse well. If the dog looks yellow around the legs, or any other place, use your whitening shampoo as a second shampoo, but do not dilute it; allow it to remain on the coat for about three minutes before rinsing out.

All wrapped up! Ch. Martin's Chanel-Cid, bred, owned, and photographed by Marjorie Martin, Columbus, Ohio.

Brush and blow-dry the dog, one section at a time, keeping a towel around the rest of the dog so that the coat will not dry out too quickly. Be sure that the temperature of the dryer is a comfortable one and not too hot; then brush as the coat dries. Work again this time with the underparts of the body first, then the legs and on to the sides, and then the head. When you have completely finished brushing and blow-drying, run the comb carefully through all parts of the coat, making absolutely certain that no mats remain undetected. *Caution! Do not ever* leave your Maltese unsupervised or alone with a hair dryer blowing on him. Should it become too hot for the dog in your absence, tragedy might well result!

The mighty Ch. Rebecca's Desert Valentino sporting the "natural braid look" as he relaxes at home between dog shows. America's # 1 Maltese for 1981 and 1982, he is owned by Freda and Rebecca Tinsley, Scottsdale, Arizona.

Ch. Mike-Mar's My Twilight Dream handled by Jane Forsyth for Dr. Kenneth Knopf, Samantha's Maltese.

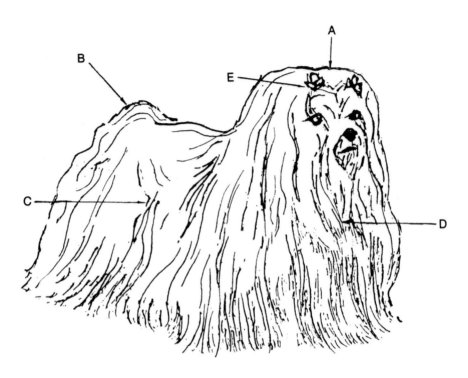

Grooming chart (courtesy of Anna Mae Hardy): A. Top of head; B. Onset of tail; C. Side of body; D. Bib; E. Top of ear.

Using a fine knitting needle, part the hair down the center of the back from the top of the head (**A** on the diagram) to the onset of tail (**B**). Make certain, of course, that this part is correctly placed running along the center of the topline, clear and distinct. Working toward the head, brush the hair on either side of the part straight down the sides of the dog (**C**), holding the top layer away with your hand as you do so and brushing a portion at a time until you have all of the side coat smooth and even. Run the comb through again now, to check that not a single mat exists.

Brush the bib straight down (**D**) using this same process from underneath the chin to the feet. Then brush out the tail (**B**).

To do the top knot, make a part starting from the corner of the eye to the top of the ear (**E**) and then from the top of the ear to the center part (**A**). Hold the hair firmly, raising it above the head, and wrap a small rubber band around it two times. Then repeat on the other side. Next take a small portion of the back hair on each side and gently pull it back, this to loosen the tightness and make a pouf. Wrap an endpaper around each side, fold back, and put a larger rubber band around each side twice, next adding a bow. More informally, to wear at home (and some exhibitors show them this way) do not part in the middle but take the entire top knot as one piece, wrap a rubber band twice around it, and pull the back portion of the hair in a backward direction. Wrap an endpaper around it, and then use a large rubber band. Be sure that you are not pulling the eye and that it is not too tight to be comfortable.

When your Maltese is all spic and span, clean and ready for the show ring, many owners like to put the entire coat up in wrappers to keep it from becoming soiled or tangled. Some even keep their little dogs that way a good part of the time when at home, as it does save wear and tear on the coat and is comfortable for the dog as well, if done carefully. Use the endpapers as Mrs. Hardy has described in doing top knots. Take the hair in even sections, fold, and secure with the rubber bands. Be certain to check and make sure that no hairs are pulling or too tight.

Sometimes, when a dog is in full coat and all groomed out, owners like to braid the top hair on the head rather than do it up in a top knot.

A Maltese who has been retired following its show career or one who is kept entirely as a pet, often looks cute in a shorter style haircut, done on the order of some of the informal Poodle trims.

A fabulous front view of Dr. Kenneth Knopf's famous winner, Ch. Anna Marie's White Panther.

Chapter X
The Making of a Show Dog

If you have decided to become a show dog exhibitor, you have accepted a very real and very exciting challenge. The groundwork has been accomplished with the selection of your future show prospect. If you have purchased a puppy, we assume that you have gone through all the proper preliminaries concerning good care, which should be the same if the puppy is a pet or future show dog with a few added precautions for the latter.

General Considerations

Remember the importance of keeping your future winner in trim, top condition. Since you want him neither too fat nor too thin, his appetite for his proper diet should be guarded, and children and guests should not be permitted to constantly be feeding him "goodies." The best treat of all is a small wad of raw ground beef or a packaged dog treat. To be avoided are ice cream, cake, cookies, potato chips, and other fattening items which will cause the dog to put on weight and may additionally spoil his appetite for the proper, nourishing, well-balanced diet so essential to good health and condition.

The importance of temperament and showmanship cannot possibly be overestimated. They have put many a mediocre dog across while lack of them can ruin the career of an otherwise outstanding specimen. From the day your dog joins your family, socialize him. Keep him accustomed to being with people and to being handled by people. Encourage your friends and relatives to "go over" him as the judges will in the ring so this will not seem a strange and upsetting experience. Practice showing his "bite" (the manner in which his teeth meet) quickly and deftly. It is

Ch. So Big's Desert Delight, handled by Rebecca Tinsley, making a good win under James Walker Trullinger in 1976. This handsome little Maltese, by Ch. Rebecca's Desert So Big ex Codere's D-D's Delight, is typical of the excellent Maltese at Freda and Rebecca Tinsley's kennel in Scottsdale, Arizona.

210

quite simple to slip the lips apart with your fingers, and the puppy should be willing to accept this from you or the judge without struggle. This is also true of further mouth examination when necessary. Where the standard demands examination of the roof of the mouth and the tongue, accustom the dog to having his jaws opened wide in order for the judge to make this required examination. When missing teeth must be noted, again, teach the dog to permit his jaws to be opened wide and his side lips separated as judges will need to check them one or both of these ways.

Some judges prefer that the exhibitors display the dog's bite and other mouth features themselves. These are the considerate ones, who do not wish to chance the spreading of possible infection from dog to dog with their hands on each one's mouth—a courtesy particularly appreciated in these days of virus epidemics. But the old fashioned judges still persist in doing it themselves, so the dog should be ready for either possibility.

Take your future show dog with you in the car, thus accustoming him to riding so that he will not become carsick on the day of a dog show. He should associate pleasure and attention with going in the car, or van or motor home. Take him where it is crowded: downtown, to the shops, everywhere you go that dogs are permitted. Make the expeditions fun for him by frequent petting and words of praise; do not just ignore him as you go about your errands.

Do not overly shelter your future show dog. Instinctively you may want to keep him at home where he is safe from germs or danger. This can be foolish on two counts. The first reason is that a puppy kept away from other dogs builds up no natural immunity against all the things with which he will come in contact at dog shows, so it is wiser actually to keep him well up to date on all protective shots and then let him become accustomed to being among dogs and dog owners. Also, a dog who never is among strange people, in strange places, or among strange dogs, may grow up with a shyness or timidity of spirit that will cause you real problems as his show career draws near.

Keep your show prospect's coat in immaculate condition with frequent grooming and daily brushing. When bathing is necessary, use a mild baby shampoo or whatever the breeder of your puppy may suggest. Several of the brand-name products do an excellent job. Be sure to rinse thoroughly so as not to risk skin

Anna Katherine Nicholas giving a careful eye to Michele Perlmutter's noted Maltese, Ch. Bar None Buckaneer as she judges Best in Show at Trenton Kennel Club after he had won the Toy Group there. Dee Shepherd handling.

One of the Calvaresi's earliest Maltese winners and a foundation for later generations, Ch. Electa Pampi of Villa Malta going Best of Breed under Anna K. Nicholas at the Progressive Dog Club in 1953. Dr. Vincenzo Calvaresi handling.

Show scene during the judging of bitches the day following the National in 1980. Courtesy of Michele Perlmutter, Ghent, New York.

Ch. Simone's King Creole, bred and owned by Simone Smith, winning a Group placement at Upper Marlboro in 1979.

irritation by traces of soap left behind and protect against soap entering the eyes by a drop of castor oil in each before you lather up. Use warm water (be sure it is not uncomfortably hot or chillingly cold) and a good spray. A hair dryer is a real convenience for the heavily coated breeds and can be used for thorough drying after first blotting off the excess moisture with a turkish towel. A wad of cotton in each ear will prevent water entering the ear cavity.

Formation of mats should be watched for carefully if your breed is a heavily coated one, especially behind the ears and underneath the armpits. Toenails also should be watched and trimmed every few weeks. It is important not to permit nails to grow excessively long, as they will ruin the appearance of both the feet and pasterns.

Assuming that you will be handling the dog yourself, or even if he will be professionally handled, a few moments each day of dog show routine is important. Practice setting him up as you have seen the exhibitors do at the shows you've attended, and teach him to hold this position once you have him stacked to your satisfaction. If he is a small breed that judges examine on a table, accustom him to this. Make the learning period pleasant by being firm but lavish in your praise when he responds correctly. Teach him to gait at your side at a moderate rate on a loose lead. When you have mastered the basic essentials at home, then hunt out and join a training class for future work. Training classes are sponsored by show-giving clubs in many areas, and their popularity is steadily increasing. If you have no other way of locating one, perhaps your veterinarian would know of one through some of his other clients; but if you are sufficiently aware of the dog show world to want a show dog, you will probably be personally acquainted with other people who will share information of this type with you.

Accustom your show dog to being in a crate (which you should be doing with a pet dog as well). He should relax in his crate at the shows "between times" for his own well being and safety.

A show dog's teeth must be kept clean and free of tartar. Hard dog-biscuits can help toward this, but if tartar accumulates, see that it is removed promptly by your veterinarian. Bones are not suitable for show dogs as they tend to damage and wear down the tooth enamel.

Match Shows

Your show dog's initial experience in the ring should be in match show competition for several reasons. First, this type of event is intended as a learning experience for both the dog and the exhibitor. You will not feel embarrassed or out of place no matter how poorly your puppy may behave or how inept your attempts at handling may be, as you will find others there with the same type of problems. The important thing is that you get the puppy out and into a show ring where the two of you can practice together and learn the ropes.

Only on rare occasions is it necessary to make match show entries in advance, and even those with a pre-entry policy will usually accept entries at the door as well. Thus you need not plan several weeks ahead, as in the case with point shows, but can go when the mood strikes you. Also there is a vast difference in the cost, as match show entries only cost a few dollars while entry fees for the point shows may be over ten dollars, an amount none of us needs to waste until we have some idea of how the puppy will behave or how much more pre-show training is needed.

Match shows very frequently are judged by professional handlers who, in addition to making the awards, are happy to help new exhibitors with comments and advice on their puppies and their presentation of them. Avail yourself of all these opportunities before heading out to the sophisticated world of the point shows.

Point Shows

As previously mentioned, entries for American Kennel Club point shows must be made in advance. This must be done on an official entry blank of the show-giving club. The entry must then be filed either personally or by mail with the show superintendent or the show secretary (if the event is being run by the club members alone and a superintendent has not been hired, this information will appear on the premium list) in time to reach its destination prior to the published closing date or filling of the quota. These entries must be made carefully, must be signed by the owner of the dog or the owner's agent (your professional handler), and must be accom-

Mrs. Henry J. Kaiser, famous for her Alekai Standard Poodles, also is a keen fancier of Maltese. Here her Ch. Aennchen's Smart Dancer is winning Best in Show at the Puerto Rico Kennel Club in the early 1960's. Handled, as are all of Mrs. Kaiser's dogs, by Wendell J. Sammet.

Mrs. Wilma S. Burg, Lumberville, Pennsylvania, co-owner of the Oak Manor Kennels with Miss Rose Stahl, is shown winning First in the Toy Group at Huntington Valley in 1959 with one of their "stars," Ch. Sussi of Villa Malta, under judge Frank Downing.

Note the beautiful expression, level top-line and other fine qualities of Ch. Aennchen's Sari Dancer as she takes Best in Show at Western Pennsylvania Kennel Club in 1965. Owned by Anna Marie Stimmler, handled by her brother, Gene Stimmler. Later owned by Michael Wolf, Mike Mar Kennels. The judge is Alva Rosenberg.

panied by the entry fee; otherwise they will not be accepted. Remember that it is not when the entry leaves your hands that counts but the date of arrival at its destination. If you are relying on the mails, which are not always dependable, get the entry off well before the deadline to avoid disappointment.

A dog must be entered at a dog show in the name of the actual owner at the time of the entry closing date of that specific show. If a registered dog has been acquired by a new owner, it must be entered in the name of the new owner in any show for which entries close after the date of acquirement, regardless of whether the new owner has or has not actually received the registration certificate indicating that the dog is recorded in his name. State on the entry form whether or not transfer application has been mailed to the American Kennel Club, and it goes without saying that the latter should be attended to promptly when you purchase a registered dog.

In filling out your entry blank, type, print, or write clearly, paying particular attention to the spelling of names, correct registration numbers, and so on. Also, if there is more than one variety in your breed, be sure to indicate into which category your dog is being entered.

The Puppy Class is for dogs or bitches who are six months of age and under twelve months, were whelped in the United States, and are not champions. The age of a dog shall be calculated up to and inclusive of the first day of a show. For example, the first day a dog whelped on January 1st is eligible to compete in a Puppy Class at a show is July 1st of the same year; and he may continue to compete in Puppy Classes up to and including a show on December 31st of the same year, but he is *not* eligible to compete in a Puppy Class at a show held on or after January 1st of the following year.

The Puppy Class is the first one in which you should enter your puppy. In it a certain allowance will be made for the fact that they *are* puppies, thus an immature dog or one displaying less than perfect showmanship will be less severely penalized than, for instance, would be the case in Open. It is also quite likely that others in the class will be suffering from these problems, too. When you enter a puppy, be sure to check the classification with care, as some shows divide their Puppy Class into a 6-9 months old section and a 9-12 months old section.

The Novice Class is for dogs six months of age and over, whelped in the United States or Canada, who *prior to the official closing date for entries* have *not* won three first prizes in the Novice Class, any first prize at all in the Bred-by Exhibitor, American-bred, or Open Classes, or one or more points toward championship. The provisions for this class are confusing to many people, which is probably the reason exhibitors do not enter in it more frequently. A dog may win any number of first prizes in the Puppy Class and still retain his eligibility for Novice. He may place second, third or fourth not only in Novice on an unlimited number of occasions but also in Bred-by-Exhibitor, American-bred and Open and still remain eligible for Novice. But he may no longer be shown in Novice when he has won three blue ribbons in that class, when he has won even one blue ribbon in either Bred-by-Exhibitor, American-bred, or Open, or when he has won a single championship point.

In determining whether or not a dog is eligible for the Novice Class, keep in mind the fact that previous wins are calculated according to the official published date for closing of entries, not by the date on which you may actually have made the entry. So if in the interim, between the time you made the entry and the official closing date, your dog makes a win causing him to become ineligible for Novice, change your class *immediately* to another for which he will be eligible, preferably such as either Bred-by-Exhibitor or American-bred. To do this, you must contact the show's superintendent or secretary, at first by telephone to save time and at the same time confirm it in writing. The Novice Class always seems to have the fewest entries of any class, and therefore it is a splendid "practice ground" for you and your young dog while you are getting the "feel" of being in the ring.

Bred-by-Exhibitor Class is for dogs whelped in the United States or, if individually registered in the American Kennel Club Stud Book, for dogs whelped in Canada who are six months of age or older, are not champions, and are owned wholly or in part by the person or by the spouse of the person who was the breeder or one of the breeders of record. Dogs entered in this class must be handled in the class by an owner or by a member of the immediate family of the owner. Members of an immediate family for this purpose are husband, wife, father, mother, son, daughter, brother or sister. This is the class which is really the

The highly successful winning bitch, Ch. Brittigan's Dark Eyes, adding another Best in Show to her record at Plainfield Kennel Club, May 1957. Owned by Mr. and Mrs. Stewart Pendleton of Ohio.

Ch. Sanibel Jessica Tate, bred and owned by Manya Dujardin. Photo courtesy of Mr. Terence Childs.

Ch. Nyssamead's Dhugal, owner handled, was a consistent winner in Eastern Maltese competition around the early 1970s. Owned by Mrs. Claudette Lemay.

Probably the most famous team of show dogs in U.S.A. history. Dr. Vincenzo Calvaresi swept the boards with his Maltese at America's most prestigious events of the 1950's and early 60's. Left to right, Ch. Ricco of Villa Malta, Ch. Rudi of Villa Malta, Ch. Renee of Villa Malta and Ceto of Villa Malta are taking a Best Team award at Westminster Kennel Club in 1957, where Mrs. Beatrice Hopkins Godsol was the judge.

"breeders' showcase," and the one which breeders should enter with particular pride to show off their achievements.

The American-bred Class is for all dogs excepting champions, six months of age or older, who were whelped in the United States by reason of a mating which took place in the United States.

The Open Class is for any dog six months of age or older (this is the only restriction for this class). Dogs with championship points compete in it, dogs who are already champions are eligible to do so, dogs who are imported can be entered, and, of course, American-bred dogs compete in it. This class is, for some strange reason, the favorite of exhibitors who are "out to win." They rush to enter their pointed dogs in it, under the false impression that by doing so they assure themselves of greater attention from the judges. This really is not so, and in my opinion to enter in one of the less competitive classes, with a better chance of winning it and thus earning a second opportunity of gaining the judge's approval by returning to the ring in the Winners Class, can often be a more effective strategy.

One does not enter for the Winners Class. One earns the right to compete in it by winning first prize in Puppy, Novice, Bred-by-Exhibitor, American-bred, or Open. No dog who has been defeated on the same day in one of these classes is eligible to compete for Winners, and every dog who has been a blue-ribbon winner in one of them and not defeated in another, should he have been entered in more than one class, (as occasionally happens) *must* do so. Following the selection of the Winners Dog or the Winners Bitch, the dog or bitch receiving that award leaves the ring. Then the dog or bitch who placed second in that class, unless previously beaten by another dog or bitch in another class at the same show, re-enters the ring to compete against the remaining first-prize winners for Reserve. The latter award indicates that the dog or bitch selected for it is standing "in reserve" should the one who received Winners be disqualified or declared ineligible through any technicality when the awards are checked at the American Kennel Club. In that case, the one who placed Reserve is moved up to Winners, at the same time receiving the appropriate championship points.

Winners Dog and Winners Bitch are the awards which carry points toward championship with them. The points are based on the number of dogs or bitches actually in competition, and the points are scaled one through five, the latter being the greatest number available to any one dog or bitch at any one show. Three-, four-, or five-point wins are considered majors. In order to become a champion, a dog or bitch must have won two majors under two different judges, plus at least one point from a third judge, and the additional points necessary to bring the total to fifteen. When your dog has gained fifteen points as described above, a championship certificate will be issued to you, and your dog's name will be published in the champions of record list in the *Pure-Bred Dogs, American Kennel Gazette,* the official publication of the American Kennel Club.

The scale of championship points for each breed is worked out by the American Kennel Club and reviewed annually, at which time the number required in competition may be either changed (raised or lowered) or remain the same. The scale of championship points for all breeds is published annually in the May issue of the *Gazette,* and the current ratings for each breed within that area are published in every show catalog.

When a dog or bitch is adjudged Best of Winners, its championship points are, for that show, compiled on the basis of which sex had the greater number of points. If there are two points in dogs and four in bitches and the dog goes Best of Winners, then *both* the dog and the bitch are awarded an equal number of points, in this case four. Should the Winners Dog or the Winners Bitch go on to win Best of Breed or Best of Variety, additional points are accorded for the additional dogs and bitches defeated by so doing, provided, of course, that there were entries specifically for Best of Breed Competition or Specials, as these specific entries are generally called.

If your dog or bitch takes Best of Opposite Sex after going Winners, points are credited according to the number of the same sex defeated in both the regular classes and Specials competition. If Best of Winners is also won, then whatever additional points for each of these awards are available will be credited. Many a one- or two-point win has grown into a major in this manner.

Moving further along, should your dog win its Variety Group from the classes (in other words, if it has taken either Winners Dog or Winners Bitch), you then receive points based on the greatest number of points awarded to any member of any breed included within that Group during that show's competition. Should

The great Ch. Rebecca's Desert Valentino, handled by Don and Pat Rodgers, was # 1 Maltese in 1981 and in 1982 was again # 1 Maltese plus # 2 Toy Dog and # 22 All Breeds. Sired by Rebecca's Desert Mr. Love ex Ch. So Big's Desert Delight, he here is winning the 1982 American Maltese Association National Specialty under judge Mrs. Frances Thornton. During May 1982, "Val" took 3 Bests in Show out of 4 on the Mission Circuit. Don and Pat Rodgers handlers. Freda Tinsley, Scottsdale, Arizona, breeder-owner.

Ch. Carlinda's Journey to All Star, noted Best in Show winning Maltese. owned by Joseph R. Champagne, Woodbury, Connecticut.

Ch. Lacy of Villa Malta here is taking Best in Show at the Virginia Kennel Club in April 1960 for owner, Mrs. Alma L. Statum, handled by Margaret M. Rozik. Villa Malta produced many a Best in Show dog, and their quality was unmistakable as one studies their various pictures.

A lovely portrait of the famed Ch. Joanne-Chen's Mino Maya Dancer, winner of 150 Toy Groups, # 1 Toy Dog, Quaker Oats System, 1981 and # 1 Producer. Twice Best of Breed at the National Specialty, once from the Veterans Class. Handled by Daryl Martin for Blanche Tenerowicz, Bienaimee Kennels, Easthampton, Mass.

the day's winning also include Best in Show, the same rule of thumb applies, and your dog or bitch receives the highest number of points awarded to any other dog of any breed at that event.

Best of Breed competition consists of the Winners Dog and the Winners Bitch, who automatically compete on the strength of those awards, in addition to whatever dogs and bitches have been entered specifically for this class for which champions of record are eligible. Since July 1980, dogs who, according to their owner's records, have completed the requirements for a championship after the closing of entries for the show, but whose championships are unconfirmed, may be transferred from one of the regular classes to the Best of Breed competition, provided this transfer is made by the show superintendent or show secretary *prior to the start of any judging at the show.*

This has proved an extremely popular new rule, as under it a dog can finish on Saturday and then be transferred and compete as a Special on Sunday. It must be emphasized that the change *must* be made *prior* to the start of *any* part of the day's judging, not for just your individual breed.

In the United States, Best of Breed winners are entitled to compete in the Variety Group which includes them. This is not mandatory, it is a privilege which exhibitors value. (In Canada, Best of Breed winners *must* compete in the Variety Group, or they lose any points already won.) The dogs winning *first* in each of the seven Variety Groups *must* compete for Best in Show. Missing the opportunity of taking your dog in for competition in its Group is foolish as it is there where the general public is most likely to notice your breed and become interested in learning about it.

Line-up of bitches at the 1980 National Specialty, courtesy of Michele Perlmutter, Bar None Kennels, Ghent, New York.

Ch. Rebecca's Desert Mr. Hearts, a litter brother to the mighty Ch. Rebecca's Desert Valentino, is another to have quickly gained titular honors. Bred and owned by Rebecca's Maltese, Scottsdale, Arizona.

Ch. Joanne-Chen's Mino Maya Dancer, owned by Blanche Tenerowicz, Bienaimee Kennels, and handled by Daryl Martin broke the record for Maltese when he gained his 150th Best in Toy Group win. He was also the winner of the Quaker Oats Award for # 1 Toy Dog for 1981, and was the only Toy dog that was both # 1 Toy Dog and # 1 Producer. Maya Dancer is the only Maltese to date to have won the American Maltese Association National Specialty from the Veterans Class, and he has won the National twice. Daryl was the youngest person ever to be presented with the Quaker Oats Award.

Ch. Oak Ridge Illusive Dream (Ch. Oak Ridge Country Charmer ex Ch. Lolarry's Chantilly Lace). Carol A. Neth handling.

Non-regular classes are sometimes included at the all-breed shows, and they are almost invariably included at Specialty Shows. These include Stud Dog Class and Brood Bitch Class, which are judged on the basis of the quality of the two offspring accompanying the sire or dam. The quality of the latter two is beside the point and should not be considered by the judge; it is the youngsters who count, and the quality of *both* are to be averaged to decide which sire or dam is the best and most consistent producer. Then there is the Brace Class (which, at all-breed shows, moves up to Best Brace in each Variety Group and then Best Brace in Show), which is judged on the similarity and evenness of appearance of the two members of the brace. In other words, the two dogs should look like identical twins in size, color, and conformation and should move together almost as a single dog, one person handling with precision and ease. The same applies to the Team Class competition, except that four dogs are involved and, if necessary, two handlers.

The Veterans Class is for the older dogs, the minimum age of whom is seven years. This class is judged on the quality of the dogs, as the winner competes in Best of Breed competition and has, on a respectable number of occasions, been known to take that top award. So the point is *not* to pick out the oldest dog, as some judges seem to believe, but the best specimen of the breed, exactly as in the regular classes.

Then there are Sweepstakes and Futurity Stakes sponsored by many Specialty clubs, sometimes as part of their regular Specialty Shows and sometimes as separate events on an entirely different occasion. The difference between the two stakes is that Sweepstakes entries usually include dogs from six to eighteen months age with entries made at the same time as the others for the show, while for a Futurity the entries are bitches nominated when bred and the individual puppies entered at or shortly following their birth.

If you already show your dog, if you plan on being an exhibitor in the future, or if you simply enjoy attending dog shows, there is a book, written by me, which you will find to be an invaluable source of detailed information about all aspects of show dog competition. This book is *Successful Dog Show Exhibiting* (T.F.H. Publications, Inc.) and is available wherever the one you are reading was purchased.

Ch. Rebecca's Desert Valentino sitting in his Best in Show trophy, one of many he has won: # 1 Maltese, U.S.A., 1981 and 1982. # 2 Toy Dog and # 22 All Breeds. By Rebecca's Desert Mr. Love ex Ch. So Big's Desert Delight. Bred and owned by Mrs. Freda Tinsley, Scottsdale, Arizona.

This is "Missy", Ch. So Big's Desert Delight, relaxed and beautiful, depicting all the charm of her enchanting breed. Freda Tinsley, owner, Rebecca's Maltese, Scottsdale, Arizona.

Wendy Neth, Carol and Tom's young daughter, is a noted "star" in Junior Showmanship. Here she is winning Best Junior Handler at Licking River Kennel Club with Ch. Oak Ridge Feather Duster. Top Maltese Junior Handler in 1979, 1980 and 1981, Wendy began helping her mother show at a very early age and has done well in the regular classes as well as in Junior competition.

Junior Showmanship Competition

If there is a youngster in your family between the ages of ten and sixteen, I can suggest no better or more rewarding hobby than becoming an active participant in Junior Showmanship. This is a marvelous activity for young people. It teaches responsibility, good sportsmanship, the fun of competition where one's own skills are the deciding factor of success, proper care of a pet, and how to socialize with other young folks. Any youngster may experience the thrill of emerging from the ring a winner and the satisfaction of a good job well done.

Entry in Junior Showmanship Classes is open to any boy or girl who is at least ten years old and under seventeen years old on the day of the show. The Novice Junior Showmanship Class is open to youngsters who have not already won, at the time the entries close, three firsts in this class. Youngsters who have won three firsts in Novice may compete in the Open Junior Showmanship Class. Any junior handler who wins his third first-place award in Novice may participate in the Open Class at the same show, provided that the Open Class has at least one other junior handler entered and competing in it that day. The Novice and Open Classes may be divided into Junior and Senior Classes. Youngsters between the ages of ten and twelve, inclusively, are eligible for the Junior division; and youngsters between thirteen and seventeen, inclusively, are eligible for the Senior division.

Any of the foregoing classes may be separated into individual classes for boys and for girls. If such a division is made, it must be so indicated on the premium list. The premium list also indicates the prize for Best Junior Handler, if such a prize is being offered at the show. Any youngster who wins a first in any of the regular classes may enter the competition for this prize, provided the youngster has been undefeated in any other Junior Showmanship Class at that show.

Junior Showmanship Classes, unlike regular conformation classes in which the quality of the dog is judged, are judged solely on the skill and ability of the junior handling the dog. Which dog is best is not the point—it is which youngster does the best job with the dog that is under consideration. Eligibility requirements for the dog being shown in Junior Showmanship, and other detailed information, can be found in *Regulations for Junior Showmanship*, available from the American Kennel Club.

This is "Charley," owned by Anna Le Blanc, going through to finish with Best of Breed and a "major" under Dee Shepherd's handling in April 1977.

Ch. Simone's Chemin De Fer, bred and owned by Simone Smith. Photo courtesy of Mr. Terence Childs.

The Tinsleys—Freda and Rebecca—were there when Ch. Rebecca's Desert Valentino won Best in Show at Superstition Kennel Club. That's Freda exchanging a kiss with him as Rebecca smiles happily and handler Don Rodgers keeps a firm hand on the lead. Freda and Rebecca co-own "Val" and he is a homebred, which has certainly brought tremendous honor to their Scottsdale, Arizona, kennels!

A junior who has a dog that he or she can enter in both Junior Showmanship and conformation classes has twice the opportunity for success and twice the opportunity to get into the ring and work with the dog, a combination which can lead to not only awards for expert handling but also, if the dog is of sufficient quality, for making a conformation champion.

Pre-Show Preparations for Your Dog and You

Preparation of the items you will need as a dog show exhibitor should not be left until the last moment. They should be planned and arranged for at least several days in advance of the show in order for you to remain calm and relaxed as the countdown starts.

The importance of the crate has already been mentioned, and we hope it is already part of your equipment. Of equal importance is the grooming table, which very likely you have also already acquired for use at home. You should take it along with you to the shows, as your dog will need last minute touches before entering the ring. Should you have not yet made this purchase, folding tables with rubber tops are made specifically for this purpose and can be purchased at most dog shows, where concession booths with marvelous assortments of "doggy" necessities are to be found, or at your pet supplier. You will also need a sturdy tack box (also available at the dog show concessions) in which to carry your grooming tools and equipment. The latter should include brushes, comb, scissors, nail clippers, whatever you use for last minute clean-up jobs, cotton swabs, first-aid equipment, and anything you are in the habit of using on the dog, including a leash or two of the type you prefer, some well-cooked and dried-out liver or any of the small packaged "dog treats" for use as bait in the ring, an atomizer in case you wish to dampen your dog's coat when you are preparing him for the ring, and so on. A large turkish towel to spread under the dog on the grooming table is also useful.

Take a large thermos or cooler of ice, the biggest one you can accommodate in your vehicle, for use by "man and beast." Take a jug of water (there are lightweight, inexpensive ones available

Ch. Martin's Christel-
Cid, by Ch. Martin's
Michael-Cid ex
Chris's Sugar, bred,
owned, and handled
by Marjorie Martin,
Martin's Maltese, Col-
umbus, Ohio

Ch. Su-Le's Nightengale, another fine winner from Barbara Bergquist's noted kennel at New Boston, Michigan.

at all sporting goods shops) and a water dish. If you plan to feed the dog at the show, or if you and the dog will be away from home more than one day, bring food for him from home so that he will have the type to which he is accustomed.

You may or may not have an exercise pen. Personally I think one a *must*, even if you only have one dog. While the shows do provide areas for the exercise of the dogs, these are among the most likely places to have your dog come in contact with any illnesses which may be going around, and I feel that having a pen of your own for your dog's use is excellent protection. Such a pen can be used in other ways, too, such as a place other than the crate in which to put the dog to relax (that is roomier than the crate) and a place in which the dog can exercise at motels and rest areas. These, too, are available at the show concession stands and come in a variety of heights and sizes. A set of "pooper scoopers" should also be part of your equipment, along with a package of plastic bags for cleaning up after your dog.

Bring along folding chairs for the members of your party, unless all of you are fond of standing, as these are almost never provided anymore by the clubs. Have your name stamped on the chairs so that there will be no doubt as to whom the chairs belong. Bring whatever you and your family enjoy for drinks or snacks in a picnic basket or cooler, as show food, in general, is expensive and usually not great. You should always have a pair of boots, a raincoat, and a rain hat with you (they should remain permanently in your vehicle if you plan to attend shows regularly), as well as a sweater, a warm coat, and a change of shoes. A smock or big cover-up apron will assure that you remain tidy as you prepare the dog for the ring. Your overnight case should include a small sewing kit for emergency repairs, bandaids, headache and indigestion remedies, and any personal products or medications you normally use.

In your car you should always carry maps of the area where you are headed and an assortment of motel directories. Generally speaking, we have found Holiday Inns to be the nicest about taking dogs. Ramadas and Howard Johnsons generally do so cheerfully (with a few exceptions). Best Western generally frowns on pets (not always, but often enough to make it necessary to find out which do). Some of the smaller chains welcome pets. The majority of privately owned motels do not.

Ch. Joanne-Chen's Maya Dancer belonged to Mamie R. Gregory and had a victorious show career under Peggy Hogg's handling. Here going Best in Show, judge, Mrs. Evers, in South Carolina on February 18th 1972.

239

The famous Ch. Our Enterprising Bebe, an important winner of the early 1980s, resting atop her crate waiting for show time. Owned by Susan Grubb, handled by Annette Lurton.

Have everything prepared the night before the show to expedite your departure. Be sure that the dog's identification and your judging program and other show information are in your purse or briefcase. If you are taking sandwiches, have them ready. Anything that goes into the car the night before the show will be one thing less to remember in the morning. Decide upon what you will wear and have it out and ready. If there is any question in your mind about what to wear, try on the possibilities before the day of the show; don't risk feeling you may want to change when you see yourself dressed a few moments prior to departure time!

In planning your outfit, make it something simple that will not detract from your dog. Remember that a dark dog silhouettes attractively against a light background and vice-versa. Sport clothes always seem to look best at dog shows, preferably conservative in type and not overly "loud" as you do not want to detract from your dog, who should be the focus of interest at this point. What you wear on your feet is important. Many types of flooring can be hazardously slippery, as can wet grass. Make it a habit to wear rubber soles and low or flat heels in the ring for your own safety, especially if you are showing a dog that likes to move out smartly.

Your final step in pre-show preparation is to leave yourself plenty of time to reach the show that morning. Traffic can get amazingly heavy as one nears the immediate area of the show, finding a parking place can be difficult, and other delays may occur. You'll be in better humor to enjoy the day if your trip to the show is not fraught with panic over fear of not arriving in time!

Enjoying the Dog Show

From the moment of your arrival at the show until after your dog has been judged, keep foremost in your mind the fact that he is your reason for being there and that he should therefore be the center of your attention. Arrive early enough to have time for those last-minute touches that can make such a great difference when he enters the ring. Be sure that he has ample time to exercise and that he attends to personal matters. A dog arriving in the ring and immediately using it as an exercise pen hardly makes a favorable impression on the judge.

When you reach ringside, ask the steward for your arm-card and anchor it firmly into place on your arm. Make sure that you are where you should be when your class is called. The fact that you have picked up your arm-card does not guarantee, as some seem to think, that the judge will wait for you. The judge has a full schedule which he wishes to complete on time. Even though you may be nervous, assume an air of calm self-confidence. Remember that this is a hobby to be enjoyed, so approach it in that state of mind. The dog will do better, too, as he will be quick to reflect your attitude.

Always show your dog with an air of pride. If you make mistakes in presenting him, don't worry about it. Next time you will do better. Do not permit the presence of more experienced exhibitors to intimidate you. After all, they, too, once were newcomers.

Ch. Su-Le's Mynah II, owned by Elyse R. Fischer and Kathy Di Giacomo.

The judging routine usually starts when the judge asks that the dogs be gaited in a circle around the ring. During this period the judge is watching each dog as it moves, noting style, topline, reach and drive, head and tail carriage, and general balance. Keep your mind and your eye on your dog, moving him at his most becoming gait and keeping your place in line without coming too close to the exhibitor ahead of you. Always keep your dog on the inside of the circle, between yourself and the judge, so that the judge's view of the dog is unobstructed.

Calmly pose the dog when requested to set up for examination whether on the ground or on a table. If you are at the head of the line and many dogs are in class, go all the way to the end of the ring before starting to stack the dog, leaving sufficient space for those behind you to line theirs up as well as requested by the judge. If you are not at the head of the line but between other exhibitors, leave sufficient space ahead of your dog for the judge to

242

examine him. The dogs should be spaced so that the judge is able to move among them to see them from all angles. In practicing to "set up" or "stack" your dog for the judge's examination, bear in mind the importance of doing so quickly and with dexterity. The judge has a schedule to meet and only a few moments in which to evaluate each dog. You will immeasurably help yours to make a favorable impression if you are able to "get it all together" in a minimum amount of time. Practice at home before a mirror can be a great help toward bringing this about, facing the dog so that you see him from the same side that the judge will and working to make him look right in the shortest length of time.

Listen carefully as the judge describes the manner in which the dog is to be gaited, whether it is straight down and straight back; down the ring, across, and back; or in a triangle. The latter has become the most popular pattern with the majority of judges. "In a triangle" means the dog should move down the outer side of the ring to the first corner, across that end of the ring to the second corner, and then back to the judge from the second cor-

Villa Norma's Charisma, handled by Wendell Sammet, won the breed from Ed Dixon.

BEST OF BREED

GILBERT PHOTO

243

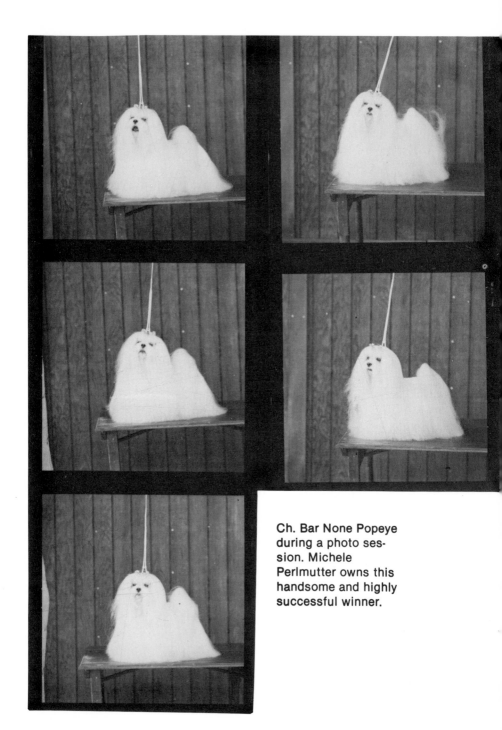

Ch. Bar None Popeye during a photo session. Michele Perlmutter owns this handsome and highly successful winner.

ner, using the center of the ring in a diagonal line. Please learn to do this pattern without breaking at each corner to twirl the dog around you, a senseless maneuver we sometimes have noted. Judges like to see the dog in an uninterrupted triangle, as they are thus able to get a better idea of the dog's gait.

It is impossible to overemphasize that the gait at which you move your dog is tremendously important, and considerable study and thought should be given to the matter. At home, have someone move the dog for you at different speeds so that you can tell which shows him off to best advantage. The most becoming action almost invariably is seen at a moderate gait, head up and topline holding. Do not gallop your dog around the ring or hurry him into a speed atypical of his breed. Nothing being rushed appears at its best; give your dog a chance to move along at his (and the breed's) natural gait. For a dog's action to be judged accurately, that dog should move with strength and power but not excessive speed, holding a straight line as he goes to and from the judge.

As you bring the dog back to the judge, stop him a few feet away and be sure that he is standing in a becoming position. Bait him to show the judge an alert expression, using whatever tasty morsel he has been trained to expect for this purpose or, if that works better for you, use a small squeak-toy in your hand. A reminder, please, to those using liver or treats. Take them with you when you leave the ring. Do not just drop them on the ground where they will be found by another dog.

When the awards have been made, accept yours graciously, no matter how you actually may feel about it. What's done is done, and arguing with a judge or stomping out of the ring is useless and a reflection on your sportsmanship. Be courteous, congratulate the winner if your dog was defeated, and try not to show your disappointment. By the same token, please be a gracious winner; this, surprisingly, sometimes seems to be still more difficult.

If you already show your dog, if you plan on being an exhibitor in the future, or if you simply enjoy attending dog shows, there is a book, written by me, which you will find to be an invaluable source of detailed information about all aspects of show dog competition. This book is *Successful Dog Show Exhibiting* (T.F.H. Publications, Inc.) and is available wherever the one you are reading was purchased.

Ch. Ginger Jake, U.D., Can. C.D.X., Baha. C.D., owned by Faith Ann Maciejewski, West Allis, Wisconsin, bred by Jo Ann Dinsmore. Jake here is winning High in Trial at the National Specialty Club under Merrill Cohen in September 1979. He has won High in Trial honors in the U.S., Canada and the Bahamas, and has been Top Maltese in Obedience in the U.S. in 1980, 1981 and 1982.

Chapter XI
Your Dog and Obedience

For its own protection and safety, every dog should be taught, at the very least, to recognize and obey the commands "Come," "Heel," "Down," "Sit," and "Stay." Doing so at some time might save the dog's life and in less extreme circumstances will certainly make him a better behaved, more pleasant member of society. If you are patient and enjoy working with your dog, study some of the excellent books available on the subject of obedience and then teach your canine friend these basic manners. If you need the stimulus of working with a group, find out where obedience training classes are held (usually your veterinarian, your dog's breeder, or a dog-owning friend can tell you) and you and your dog can join up. Alternatively, you could let someone else do the training by sending the dog to class, but this is not very rewarding because you lose the opportunity of working with your dog and the pleasure of the rapport thus established.

If you are going to do it yourself, there are some basic rules which you should follow. You must remain calm and confident in attitude. Never lose your temper and frighten or punish your dog unjustly. Be quick and lavish with praise each time a command is correctly followed. Make it fun for the dog and he will be eager to please you by responding correctly. Repetition is the keynote, but it should not be continued without recess to the point of tedium. Limit the training sessions to ten- or fifteen-minute periods at a time.

Formal obedience training can be followed, and very frequently is, by entering the dog in obedience competition to work toward an obedience degree, or several of them, depending on the dog's aptitude and your own enjoyment. Obedience trials are held in conjunction with the majority of all-breed conformation dog shows, with Specialty shows, and frequently as separate Specialty events. If you are working alone with your dog, a list of

Showing the excellent form which has made him so successful a winner, Ch. Ginger Jake, U.S. U.D., Can. C.D.X. and Baha. C.D. takes a jump with ease. Breeder Jo Ann Dinsmore comments "Maltese are easy to train, and fun."

trial dates might be obtained from your dog's veterinarian, your dog breeder, or a dog-owning friend; the A.K.C. *Gazette* lists shows and trials to be scheduled in the coming months; and if you are a member of a training class, you will find the information readily available.

The goals for which one works in the formal A.K.C. Member or Licensed Trials are the following titles: Companion Dog (C.D.), Companion Dog Excellent (C.D.X.), and Utility Dog (U.D.). These degrees are earned by receiving three "legs," or qualifying scores, at each level of competition. The degrees must be earned in order, with one completed prior to starting work on the next. For example, a dog must have earned C.D. prior to starting work on C.D.X.; then C.D.X. must be completed before U.D. work begins. The ultimate title attainable in obedience work is Obedience Trial Champion (O.T.Ch.).

When you see the letters "C.D." following a dog's name, you will know that this dog has satisfactorily completed the following exercises: heel on leash, heel free, stand for examination, recall, long sit and long stay. "C.D.X." means that tests have been passed on all of those just mentioned plus heel free, drop on recall, retrieve over high jump, broad jump, long sit, and long down. "U.D." indicates that the dog has additionally passed tests in scent discrimination (leather article), scent discrimination (metal article), signal exercises, directed retrieve, directed jumping, and group stand for examination. The letters "O.T.Ch." are the abbreviation for the only obedience title which precedes rather than follows a dog's name. To gain an obedience trial championship, a dog who already holds a Utility Dog degree must win a total of one hundred points and must win three firsts, under three different judges, in Utility and Open B Classes.

There is also a Tracking Dog title (T.D.) which can be earned at tracking trials. In order to pass the tracking tests the dog must follow the trail of a stranger along a path on which the trail was laid between thirty minutes and two hours previously. Along this track there must be more than two right-angle turns, at least two of which are well out in the open where no fences or other boundaries exist for the guidance of the dog or the handler. The dog wears a harness and is connected to the handler by a lead twenty to forty feet in length. Inconspicuously dropped at the end of the track is an article to be retrieved, usually a glove or wallet, which the dog is expected to locate and the handler to pick up. The letters "T.D.X." is the abbreviation for Tracking Dog Excellent, more difficult version of the Tracking Dog test with a longer track and more turns to be worked through.

Ch. Martin's Mina Puff is the dam of several champions as well as a well-known winner. Handled by Daryl Martin for Blanche Tenerowicz, Bienaimee Maltese, Easthampton, Mass.

Chapter XII
Breeding Your Maltese

The Maltese Brood Bitch

We have in an earlier chapter discussed selection of a bitch you plan to use for breeding. In making this important purchase, you will be choosing a bitch who you hope will become the foundation of your kennel. Thus she must be of the finest producing bloodlines, excellent in temperament, of good type, and free of major faults or unsoundness. If you are offered a "bargain" brood bitch, be wary, as for this purchase you should not settle for less than the best and the price will be in accordance with the quality.

Conscientious breeders feel quite strongly that the only possible reason for producing puppies is the ambition to improve and uphold quality and temperament within the breed—definitely *not* because one hopes to make a quick cash profit on a mediocre litter, which never seems to work out that way in the long run and which accomplishes little beyond perhaps adding to the nation's heartbreaking number of unwanted canines. The only reason ever for breeding a litter is, with conscientious people, a desire to improve the quality of dogs in their own kennel or, as pet owners, because they wish to add to the number of dogs they themselves own with a puppy or two from their present favorites. In either case breeding should not take place unless one has definitely prospective owners for as many puppies as the litter may contain, lest you find yourself with several fast-growing young dogs and no homes in which to place them.

Bitches should not be mated earlier than their second season, by which time they should be from fifteen to eighteen months old. Many breeders prefer to wait and first finish the championships of their show bitches before breeding them, as pregnancy can be a disaster to a show coat and getting the bitch back in shape again takes time. When you have decided what will be the proper time, start watching at least several months ahead for

251

Allan's Rosebud, the dam of Ch. Michael-Cid, owned and photographed by Marjorie Martin, Martin's Maltese, Columbus, Ohio.

what you feel would be the perfect mate to best complement your bitch's quality and bloodlines. Subscribe to the magazines which feature your breed exclusively and to some which cover all breeds in order to familiarize yourself with outstanding stud dogs in areas other than your own for there is no necessity nowadays to limit your choice to a nearby dog unless you truly like him and feel that he is the most suitable. It is quite usual to ship a bitch to a stud dog a distance away, and this generally works out with no ill effects. The important thing is that you need a stud dog strong in those features where your bitch is weak or lacking and of bloodlines compatible to hers. Compare the background of both your bitch and the stud dog under consideration, paying particular attention to the quality of the puppies from bitches with backgrounds similar to your bitch's. If the puppies have been of the type and quality you admire, then this dog would seem a sensible choice for yours, too.

Stud fees may be a few hundred dollars, sometimes even more under special situations for a particularly successful sire. It is money well spent, however. Do *not* ever breed to a dog because he is less expensive than the others unless you honestly believe that he can sire the kind of puppies who will be a credit to your kennel and your breed.

Contacting the owners of the stud dogs you find interesting will bring you pedigrees and pictures which you can then study in relation to your bitch's pedigree and conformation. Discuss your plans with other breeders who are knowledgeable (including the one who bred your own bitch). You may not always receive an entirely unbiased opinion (particularly if the person giving it also has an available stud dog), but one learns by discussion so listen to what they say, consider their opinions, and then you may be better qualified to form your own opinion.

As soon as you have made a choice, phone the owner of the stud dog you wish to use to find out if this will be agreeable. You will be asked about the bitch's health, soundness, temperament, and freedom from serious faults. A copy of her pedigree may be requested, as might a picture of her. A discussion of her background over the telephone may be sufficient to assure the stud's owner that she is suitable for the stud dog and of type, breeding, and quality herself to produce puppies of the quality for which the dog is noted. The owner of a top-quality stud is often extremely selective in the bitches permitted to be bred to his dog, in an effort to keep the standard of his puppies high. The owner of a stud dog may require that the bitch be tested for brucellosis, which should be attended to not more than a month previous to the breeding.

Check out which airport will be most convenient for the person meeting and returning the bitch if she is to be shipped and also what airlines use that airport. You will find that the airlines are also apt to have special requirements concerning acceptance of animals for shipping. These include weather limitations and types of crates which are acceptable. The weather limits have to do with extreme heat and extreme cold at the point of destination, as some airlines will not fly dogs into temperatures above or below certain levels, fearing for their safety. The crate problem is a simple one, since if your own crate is not suitable, most of the airlines have specially designed crates available for purchase at a fair and moderate price. It is a good plan to purchase one of these if you intend to be shipping dogs with any sort of frequency. They are made of fiberglass and are the safest type to use for shipping.

Normally you must notify the airline several days in advance to make a reservation, as they are able to accommodate only a certain number of dogs on each flight. Plan on shipping the bitch on about her eighth or ninth day of season, but be careful to avoid shipping her on a weekend, when schedules often vary and freight offices are apt to be closed. Whenever you can, ship your bitch on a direct flight. Changing planes always carries a certain amount of risk of a dog being overlooked or wrongly routed at the middle stop, so avoid this danger if at all possible. The bitch must be accompanied by a health certificate which you must obtain from your veterinarian before taking her to the airport. Usually it will be necessary to have the bitch at the airport about two hours prior to flight time. Before finalizing arrangements, find out from the stud's owner at what time of day it will be most convenient to have the bitch picked up promptly upon arrival.

It is simpler if you can plan to bring the bitch to the stud dog. Some people feel that the trauma of the flight may cause the bitch to not conceive; and, of course, undeniably there is a slight risk in shipping which can be avoided if you are able to drive the bitch to her destination. Be sure to leave yourself sufficient time to assure your arrival at the right time for her for breeding (normally the tenth to fourteenth day following the first signs of color); and remember that if you want the bitch bred twice, you should allow a day to elapse between the two matings. Do not expect the stud's owner to house you while you are there. Locate a nearby motel that takes dogs and make that your headquarters.

Just prior to the time your bitch is due in season, you should take her to visit your veterinarian. She should be checked for worms and should receive all the booster shots for which she is due plus one for parvo virus, unless she has had the latter shot fairly recently. The brucellosis test can also be done then, and the health certificate can be obtained for shipping if she is to travel by air. Should the bitch be at all overweight, now is the time to get the surplus off. She should be in good condition, neither underweight nor overweight, at the time of breeding.

The moment you notice the swelling of the vulva, for which you should be checking daily as the time for her season approaches, and the appearance of color, immediately contact the stud's owner and settle on the day for shipping or make the appointment for your arrival with the bitch for breeding. If you are shipping the bitch, the stud fee check should be mailed immediately, leaving ample time for it to have been received when the bitch arrives and the mating takes place. Be sure to call the airline making her reservation at that time, too.

Do not feed the bitch within a few hours before shipping her. Be certain that she has had a drink of water and been well exercised before closing her in the crate. Several layers of newspapers, topped with some shredded newspaper, make a good bed and can be discarded when she arrives at her destination; these can be replaced with fresh newspapers for her return home. Remember that the bitch should be brought to the airport about two hours before flight time as sometimes the airlines refuse to accept late arrivals.

If you are taking your bitch by car, be certain that you will arrive at a reasonable time of day. Do not appear late in the evening. If your arrival in town is not until late, get a good night's sleep at your motel and contact the stud's owner first thing in the morning. If possible, leave children and relatives at home, as they will only be in the way and perhaps unwelcome by the stud's owner. Most stud dog owners prefer not to have any unnecessary people on hand during the actual mating.

After the breeding has taken place, if you wish to sit and visit for awhile and the stud's owner has the time, return the bitch to her crate in your car (first ascertaining, of course, that the temperature is comfortable for her and that there is proper ventilation. She should not be permitted to urinate for at least one hour following the breeding. This is the time when you get the business part of the transaction attended to. Pay the stud fee, upon which you should receive your breeding certificate and, if you do not already have it, a copy of the stud dog's pedigree. The owner of the stud dog does not sign or furnish a litter registration application until the puppies have been born.

Upon your return home, you can settle down and plan in happy anticipation a wonderful litter of puppies. A word of caution! Remember that although she has been bred, your bitch is still an interesting target for all male dogs, so guard her carefully for the next week or until you are absolutely certain that her season has entirely ended. This would be no time to have any unfortunate incident with another dog.

The Maltese Stud Dog

Choosing the best stud dog to complement your bitch is often very difficult. The two principal factors to be considered should be the stud's conformation and his pedigree. Conformation is fairly obvious; you want a dog that is typical of the breed in the words of the standard of perfection. Understanding pedigrees is a bit more subtle since the pedigree lists the ancestry of the dog and involves individuals and bloodlines with which you may not be entirely familiar.

To a novice in the breed, then, the correct interpretation of a pedigree may at first be difficult to grasp. Study the pictures and text of this book and you will find many names of important bloodlines and members of the breed. Also make an effort to discuss the various dogs behind the proposed stud with some of the more experienced breeders, starting with the breeder of your own bitch. Frequently these folks will be personally familiar with many of the dogs in question, can offer opinions of them, and may have access to additional pictures which you would benefit by seeing.

Ch. To The Victor of Eng is an extremely important little dog in Maltese history, being the sire of 63 champions as this is written, thus the all-time Top Producer in the breed, living or dead. Owned by Barbara J. Bergquist, New Boston, Michigan.

It is very important that the stud's pedigree should be harmonious with that of the bitch you plan on breeding to him. Do not rush out and breed to the latest winner with no thought of whether or not he can produce true quality. By no means are all great show dogs great producers. It is the producing record of the dog in question and the dogs and bitches from which he has come which should be the basis on which you make your choice.

Breeding dogs is never a money-making operation. By the time you pay a stud fee, care for the bitch during pregnancy, whelp the litter, and rear the puppies through their early shots, worming, and so on, you will be fortunate to break even financially once the puppies have been sold. Your chances of doing this are greater if you are breeding for a show-quality litter which will bring you higher prices as the pups are sold as show prospects. Therefore, your wisest investment is to use the best dog available for your bitch regardless of the cost; then you should wind up with more valuable puppies. Remember that it is equally costly to raise mediocre puppies as top ones, and your chances of financial return are better on the latter. To breed to the most excellent, most suitable stud dog you can find is the only sensible thing to do, and it is poor economy to quibble over the amount you are paying in stud fee.

It will be your decision which course you decide to follow when you breed your bitch, as there are three options: line-breeding, inbreeding, and outcrossing. Each of these methods has its supporters and its detractors! Line-breeding is breeding a bitch to a dog belonging originally to the same canine family, being descended from the same ancestors, such as half-brother to half-sister, grandsire to granddaughters, niece to uncle (and vice-versa) or cousin to cousin. Inbreeding is breeding father to daughter, mother to son, or full brother to sister. Outcross breeding is breeding a dog and a bitch with no or only a few mutual ancestors.

Line-breeding is probably the safest course, and the one most likely to bring results, for the novice breeder. The more sophisticated inbreeding should be left to the experienced, long-time breeders who thoroughly know and understand the risks and the possibilities involved with a particular line. It is usually done in an effort to intensify some ideal feature in that strain. Outcrossing is the reverse of inbreeding, an effort to introduce improvement in a specific feature needing correction, such as a shorter back, better movement, more correct head or coat, and so on.

It is the serious breeder's ambition to develop a strain or bloodline of their own, one strong in qualities for which their dogs will become distinguished. However, it must be realized that this will involve time, patience, and at least several generations before the achievement can be claimed. The safest way to embark on this plan, as we have mentioned, is by the selection and breeding of one or two bitches, the best you can buy and from top-producing kennels. In the beginning you do *not* really have to own a stud dog. In the long run it is less expensive and sounder judgment to pay a stud fee when you are ready to breed a bitch than to purchase a stud dog and feed him all year; a stud dog does not win any popularity contests with owners of bitches to be bred until he becomes a champion, has been successfully Specialed for awhile, and has been at least moderately advertised, all of which adds up to a quite healthy expenditure.

The wisest course for the inexperienced breeder just starting out in dogs is as I have outlined above. Keep the best bitch puppy from the first several litters. After that you may wish to consider keeping your own stud dog if there has been a particularly handsome male in one of your litters that you feel has great potential or if you know where there is one available that you are interested in, with the feeling that he would work in nicely with the breeding program on which you have embarked. By this time, with several litters already born, your eye should have developed to a point enabling you to make a wise choice, either from one of your own litters or from among dogs you have seen that appear suitable.

The greatest care should be taken in the selection of your own stud dog. He must be of true type and highest quality as he may be responsible for siring many puppies each year, and he should come from a line of excellent dogs on both sides of his pedigree which themselves are, and which are descended from, successful producers. This dog should have no glaring faults in conformation; he should be of such quality that he can hold his own in keenest competition within his breed. He should be in good health, be virile and be a keen stud dog, a proven sire able to transmit his correct qualities to his puppies. Need I say that such a dog will be enormously expensive unless you have the good fortune to produce him in one of your own litters? To buy and use a lesser stud dog, however, is downgrading your breeding program unnecessarily since there are so many dogs fitting the description of a fine stud whose services can be used on payment of a stud fee.

You should *never* breed to an unsound dog or one with any serious standard or disqualifying faults. Not all champions by any means pass along their best features; and by the same token, occasionally you will find a great one who can pass along his best features but never gained his championship title due to some unusual circumstances. The information you need about a stud dog is what type of puppies he has produced and with what bloodlines and whether or not he possesses the bloodlines and attributes considered characteristic of the best in your breed.

If you go out to buy a stud dog, obviously he will not be a puppy but rather a fully mature and proven male with as many of the best attributes as possible. True, he will be an expensive investment, but if you choose and make his selection with care and forethought, he may well prove to be one of the best investments you have ever made.

Of course, the most exciting of all is when a young male you have decided to keep from one of your litters due to his tremendous show potential turns out to be a stud dog such as we have described. In this case he should be managed with care, for he is a valuable property that can contribute inestimably to this breed as a whole and to your own kennel specifically.

Do not permit your stud dog to be used until he is about a year old, and even then he should be bred to a mature, proven matron accustomed to breeding who will make his first experience pleasant and easy. A young dog can be put off forever by a maiden bitch who fights and resists his advances. Never allow this to happen. Always start a stud dog out with a bitch who is mature, has been bred previously, and is of even temperament. The first breeding should be performed in quiet surroundings with only you and one other person to hold the bitch. Do not make it a circus, as the experience will determine the dog's outlook about future stud work. If he does not enjoy the first experience or associates it with any unpleasantness, you may well have a problem in the future.

Your young stud must permit help with the breeding, as later there will be bitches who will not be cooperative. If right from the

These two Maltese produced the current big winner, Ch. Noble Faith's White Tornado, owned by Faith Knobel and Liz Foster. They are (left) Ch. Noble Faith's Phoebe's Finale handled by Glynette Cass and (right) Ch. Oak Ridge Country Charmer handled by Carol Neth, the dam and sire, respectively, of Tornado.

beginning you are there helping him and praising him whether or not your assistance is actually needed, he will expect and accept this as a matter of course when a difficult bitch comes along.

Things to have handy before introducing your dog and the bitch are K-Y jelly (the only lubricant which should be used) and a length of gauze with which to muzzle the bitch should it be necessary to keep her from biting you or the dog. Some bitches put up a fight; others are calm. It is best to be prepared.

At the time of the breeding the stud fee comes due, and it is expected that it will be paid promptly. Normally a return service is offered in case the bitch misses or fails to produce one live puppy. Conditions of the service are what the stud dog's owner makes them, and there are no standard rules covering this. The stud fee is paid for the act, not the result. If the bitch fails to conceive, it is customary for the owner to offer a free return service; but this is a courtesy and not to be considered a right, particularly in the case of a proven stud who is siring consistently and whose fault the failure obviously is *not*. Stud dog owners are always anxious to see their clients get good value and to have in the ring winning young stock by their dog; therefore, very few refuse to mate the second time. It is wise, however, for both parties to have the terms of the transaction clearly understood at the time of the breeding.

If the return service has been provided and the bitch has missed a second time, that is considered to be the end of the matter and the owner would be expected to pay a further fee if it is felt that the bitch should be given a third chance with the stud dog. The management of a stud dog and his visiting bitches is quite a task, and a stud fee has usually been well earned when one service has been achieved, let alone by repeated visits from the same bitch.

The accepted litter is one live puppy. It is wise to have printed a breeding certificate which the owner of the stud dog and the owner of the bitch both sign. This should list in detail the conditions of the breeding as well as the dates of the mating.

Upon occasion, arrangements other than a stud fee in cash are made for a breeding, such as the owner of the stud taking a pick-of-the-litter puppy in lieu of money. This should be clearly specified on the breeding certificate along with the terms of the age at which the stud's owner will select the puppy, whether it is to be a specific sex, or whether it is to be the pick of the entire litter.

The price of a stud fee varies according to circumstances. Usually, to prove a young stud dog, his owner will allow the first breeding to be quite inexpensive. Then, once a bitch has become pregnant by him, he becomes a "proven stud" and the fee rises accordingly for bitches that follow. The sire of championship-quality puppies will bring a stud fee of at least the purchase price of one show puppy as the accepted "rule-of-thumb." Until at least one champion by your stud dog has finished, the fee will remain equal to the price of one pet puppy. When his list of cham-

Ch. Su-Le's Crex owned by Barbara Bergquist, New Boston, Michigan.

pions starts to grow, so does the amount of the stud fee. For a top-producing sire of champions, the stud fee will rise accordingly.

Almost invariably it is the bitch who comes to the stud dog for the breeding. Immediately upon having selected the stud dog you wish to use, discuss the possibility with the owner of that dog. It is the stud dog owner's prerogative to refuse to breed any bitch deemed unsuitable for this dog. Stud fee and method of payment should be stated at this time, and a decision reached on whether it is to be a full cash transaction at the time of the mating or a pick-of-the-litter puppy, usually at eight weeks of age.

If the owner of the stud dog must travel to an airport to meet the bitch and ship her for the flight home, an additional charge will be made for time, tolls, and gasoline based on the stud owner's proximity to the airport. The stud fee includes board for the day on the bitch's arrival through two days for breeding, with a day in between. If it is necessary that the bitch remain longer, it is very likely that additional board will be charged at the normal per-day rate for the breed.

Ch. Su-Le's Wren of Eng, imported Maltese owned by Barbara J. Bergquist and owner-handled to the win, takes Best in Show at Memphis, Tennessee, in 1971.

This lovely bitch, Ch. Su-Le's Bunting, after winning the Best Puppy from the regular classes at the first American Maltese Ass'n. Independent National Specialty, went on to this exciting victory of Best Toy at Boardwalk Kennel Club in December 1971. Handled by Barbara Alderman for owner Barbara Bergquist, Su-Le Maltese, New Boston, Michigan.

Be sure to advise the stud's owner as soon as you know that your bitch is in season so that the stud dog will be available. This is especially important because if he is a dog being shown, he and his owner may be unavailable owing to the dog's absence from home.

As the owner of a stud dog being offered to the public, it is essential that you have proper facilities for the care of visiting bitches. Nothing can be worse than a bitch being insecurely housed and slipping out to become lost or bred by the wrong dog. If you are taking people's valued bitches into your kennel or home, it is imperative that you provide them with comfortable, secure housing and good care while they are your responsibility.

There is no dog more valuable than the proven sire of champions, Group winners and Best in Show dogs. Once you have such an animal, guard his reputation well and do *not* permit him to be bred to just any bitch that comes along. It takes two to make the puppies; even the most dominant stud can not do it all himself, so never permit him to breed a bitch you consider unworthy. Remember that when the puppies arrive, it will be your stud dog who will be blamed for any lack of quality, while the bitch's shortcomings will be quickly and conveniently overlooked.

Going into the actual management of the mating is a bit superfluous here. If you have had previous experience in breeding a dog and bitch you will know how the mating is done. If you do not have such experience, you should not attempt to follow directions given in a book but should have a veterinarian, breeder friend, or handler there to help you the first few times. You do not just turn the dog and bitch loose together and await developments, as too many things can go wrong and you may altogether miss getting the bitch bred. Someone should hold the dog and the bitch (one person each) until the "tie" is made and these two people should stay with them during the entire act.

If you get a complete tie, probably only the one mating is absolutely necessary. However, especially with a maiden bitch or one that has come a long distance for this breeding, we prefer following up with a second breeding, leaving one day in between the two matings. In this way there will be little or no chance of the bitch missing.

Once the tie has been completed and the dogs release, be certain that the male's penis goes completely back within its sheath. He should be allowed a drink of water and a short walk, and then he should be put into his crate or somewhere alone where he can settle down. Do not allow him to be with other dogs for a while as they will notice the odor of the bitch on him, and particularly with other males present, he may become involved in a fight.

Pregnancy, Whelping, and the Litter

Once the bitch has been bred and is back at home, remember to keep an ever watchful eye that no other male gets to her until at least the twenty-second day of her season has passed. Until then, it will still be possible for an unwanted breeding to take place, which at this point would be catastrophic. Remember that she actually can have two separate litters by two different dogs, so take care.

In other ways, she should be treated normally. Controlled exercise is good, and necessary for the bitch throughout her pregnancy, tapering it off to just several short walks daily, preferably on lead, as she reaches about her seventh week. As her time grows close, be careful about her jumping or playing too roughly.

The theory that a bitch should be overstuffed with food when pregnant is a poor one. A fat bitch is never an easy whelper, so the overfeeding you consider good for her may well turn out to be the exact opposite. During the first few weeks of pregnancy, your bitch should be fed her normal diet. At four to five weeks along, calcium should be added to her food. At seven weeks her food may be increased if she seems to crave more than she is getting, and a meal of canned milk (mixed with an equal amount of water) should be introduced. If she is fed just once a day, add another meal rather than overload her with too much at one time. If twice a day is her schedule, then a bit more food can be added to each feeding.

A week before the pups are due, your bitch should be introduced to her whelping box so that she will be accustomed to it and feel at home there when the puppies arrive. She should be encouraged to sleep there but permitted to come and go as she wishes. The box should be roomy enough for her to lie down and stretch out but not too large lest the pups have more room than is needed in which to roam and possibly get chilled by going too far away from their mother. Be sure that the box has a "pig rail"; this will prevent the puppies from being crushed against the

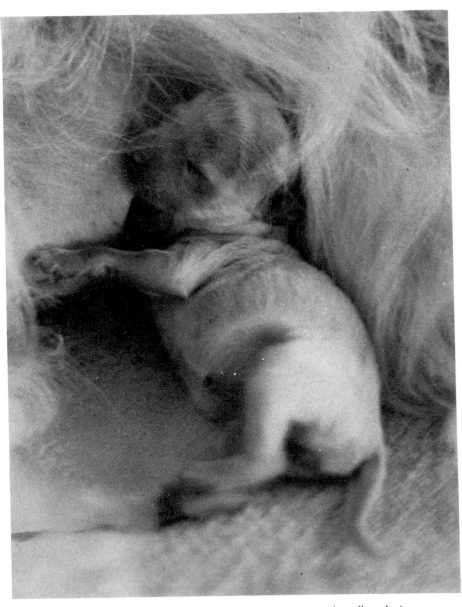

Day-old Maltese puppy, Rosebud II. Breeder-owner-handler-photographer, Marjorie Martin, Martin's Maltese, Columbus, Ohio.

An all-girl litter at Bar None Kennels, by Bar None Bilbo Baggins ex Bar None Kizzy. This is a repeat of the breeding which produced Ch. Bar None Bette Davis Eyes and Bar None The One and Only. Michele Perlmutter, owner, Ghent, New York.

sides. The room in which the box is placed, either in your home or in the kennel, should be kept at about 70 degrees Fahrenheit. In winter it may be necessary to have an infrared lamp over the whelping box, in which case be careful not to place it too low or close to the puppies.

Newspapers will become a very important commodity, so start collecting them well in advance to have a big pile handy to the whelping box. With a litter of puppies, one never seems to have papers enough, so the higher pile to start with, the better off you will be. Other necessities for whelping time are clean, soft turkish towels, scissors, and a bottle of alcohol.

You will know that her time is very near when your bitch becomes restless, wandering in and out of her box and of the room. She may refuse food, and at that point her temperature will start to drop. She will dig at and tear up the newspapers in her box, shiver, and generally look uncomfortable. Only you should be with your bitch at this time. She does not need spectators; and several people, even though they may be family members whom she knows, hanging over her may upset her to the point where she may harm the puppies. You should remain nearby, quietly watching, not fussing or hovering; speak calmly and frequently to her to instill confidence. Eventually she will settle down in her box and begin panting; contractions will follow. Soon thereafter a puppy will start to emerge, sliding out with the contractions. The mother immediately should open the sac, sever the cord with her teeth, and then clean up the puppy. She will also eat the placenta, which you should permit. Once the puppy is cleaned, it should be placed next to the bitch unless she is showing signs of having the next one immediately. Almost at once the puppy will start looking for a nipple on which to nurse, and you should ascertain that it is able to latch on successfully.

If the puppy is a breech (*i.e.,* born feet first), you must watch carefully for it to be completely delivered as quickly as possible and the sac removed quickly so that the puppy does not drown. Sometimes even a normally positioned birth will seem extremely slow in coming. Should this occur, you might take a clean towel and, as the bitch contracts, pull the puppy out, doing so gently and with utmost care. If, once the puppy is delivered, it shows little signs of life, take a rough turkish towel and massage the puppy's chest by rubbing quite briskly back and forth. Continue this for about fifteen minutes, and be sure that the mouth is free from liquid. It may be necessary to try mouth-to-mouth breathing, which is done by pressing the puppy's jaws open and, using a finger, depressing the tongue which may be stuck to the roof of the mouth. Then place your mouth against the puppy's and blow hard down the puppy's throat. Bubbles may pop out of its nose, but keep on blowing. Rub the puppy's chest with the towel again and try artificial respiration, pressing the sides of the chest together slowly and rhythmically—in and out, in and out. Keep trying one method or the other for at least twenty minutes before giving up. You may be rewarded with a live puppy who otherwise would not have made it.

If you are successful in bringing the puppy around, do not immediately put it back with the mother as it should be kept extra warm. Put it in a cardboard box on an electric heating pad or, if it is the time of year when your heat is running, near a radiator or near the fireplace or stove. As soon as the rest of the litter has been born it then can join the others.

An hour or more may elapse between puppies, which is fine so long as the bitch seems comfortable and is neither straining nor contracting. She should not be permitted to remain unassisted for more than an hour if she does continue to contract. This is when you should get her to your veterinarian, whom you should already have alerted to the possibility of a problem existing. He should examine her and perhaps give her a shot of Pituitrin. In some cases the veterinarian may find that a Caesarean section is necessary due to a puppy being lodged in a manner making normal delivery impossible. Sometimes this is caused by an abnormally large puppy, or it may just be that the puppy is simply turned in the wrong position. If the bitch does require a Caesarean section, the puppies already born must be kept warm in their cardboard box with a heating pad under the box.

Once the section is done, get the bitch and the puppies home. Do not attempt to put the puppies in with the bitch until she has regained consciousness as she may unknowingly hurt them. But do get them back to her as soon as possible for them to start nursing.

Should the mother lack milk at this time, the puppies must be fed by hand, kept very warm, and held onto the mother's teats several times a day in order to stimulate and encourage the secretion of milk, which should start shortly.

An exquisite Ben Burwell head-study of Mr. and Mrs. Henry J. Kaiser's famous winning Maltese, Ch. Aennchen's Smart Dancer.

Ch. Aennchen's Cari Krsna Dancer, by Ch. Aennchen's Soomi Dancer ex Cari Joanne-Chen's Munchkin, is an unusually excellent producer of quality puppies, and had whelped two litters prior to starting her successful show career. Owned and handled by Nicholas Cutillo, New York City.

Assuming that there has been no problem and that the bitch has whelped naturally, you should insist that she go out to exercise, staying just long enough to make herself comfortable. She can be offered a bowl of milk and a biscuit, but then she should settle down with her family. Freshen the whelping box for her with fresh newspapers while she is taking this respite so that she and the puppies will have a clean bed.

Unless some problem arises, there is little you must do about the puppies until they become three to four weeks old. Keep the box clean and supplied with fresh newspapers the first few days, but then turkish towels should be tacked down to the bottom of the box so that the puppies will have traction as they move about.

If the bitch has difficulties with her milk supply, or if you should be so unfortunate as to lose her, then you must be prepared to either hand-feed or tube-feed the puppies if they are to survive. We personally prefer tube-feeding as it is so much faster and easier. If the bitch is available, it is best that she continues to clean and care for the puppies in the normal manner excepting for the food supplements you will provide. If it is impossible for her to do this, then after every feeding you must gently rub each puppy's abdomen with wet cotton to make it urinate, and the rectum should be gently rubbed to open the bowels.

Newborn puppies must be fed every three to four hours around the clock. The puppies must be kept warm during this time. Have your veterinarian teach you how to tube-feed. You will find that it is really quite simple.

After a normal whelping, the bitch will require additional food to enable her to produce sufficient milk. In addition to being fed twice daily, she should be given some canned milk several times each day.

When the puppies are two weeks old, their nails should be clipped, as they are needle sharp at this age and can hurt or damage the mother's teats and stomach as the pups hold on to nurse.

Between three and four weeks of age, the puppies should begin to be weaned. Scraped beef (prepared by scraping it off slices of beef with a spoon so that none of the gristle is included) may be offered in very small quantities a couple of times daily for the first few days. Then by the third day you can mix puppy chow with warm water as directed on the package, offering it four times daily. By now the mother should be kept away from the puppies and out of the box for several hours at a time so that when they have reached five weeks of age she is left in with them only overnight. By the time the puppies are six weeks old, they should be entirely weaned and receiving only occasional visits from their mother.

Most veterinarians recommend a temporary DHL (distemper, hepatitis, leptospirosis) shot when the puppies are six weeks of age. This remains effective for about two weeks. Then at eight weeks of age, the puppies should receive the series of permanent shots for DHL protection. It is also a good idea to discuss with your vet the advisability of having your puppies inoculated against the dreaded parvovirus at the same time. Each time the

Ch. Kathan's Blu Flower of Chelsea, winning her final point at Delaware Water Gap in 1979. Owned by Gail Hennessey, Wappingers Falls, New York.

pups go to the vet for shots, you should bring stool samples so that they can be examined for worms. Worms go through various stages of development and may be present in a stool sample even though the sample does not test positive in every checkup. So do not neglect to keep careful watch on this.

The puppies should be fed four times daily until they are three months old. Then you can cut back to three feedings daily. By the time the puppies are six months of age, two meals daily are sufficient. Some people feed their dogs twice daily throughout their lifetime; others go to one meal daily when the puppy becomes one year of age.

The ideal age for puppies to go to their new homes is between eight and twelve weeks, although some puppies successfully adjust to a new home when they are six weeks old. Be sure that they go to their new owners accompanied by a description of the diet you've been feeding them and a schedule of the shots they have already received and those they still need. These should be included with the registration application and a copy of the pedigree.

The lovely multiple Best in Show winning Maltese, Ch. Our Enterprising Bebe, was a great favorite with the judges at the beginning of the 1980's. Sired by Ch. To The Victor of Eng ex Joanne Chen's Kandi Bon Bon, this stunning bitch was handled by Annette Lurton to an exciting career for owner Susan Grubb.

276

Chapter XIII
Traveling with Your Dog

When you travel with your dog, to shows or on vacation or wherever, remember that everyone does not share our enthusiasm or love for dogs and that those who do not, strange creatures though they seem to us, have their rights, too. These rights, on which we should not encroach, include not being disturbed, annoyed, or made uncomfortable by the presence and behavior of other people's pets. Your dog should be kept on lead in public places and should recognize and promptly obey the commands "Down," "Come," "Sit," and "Stay."

Take along his crate if you are going any distance with your dog. And keep him in it when riding in the car. A crated dog has a far better chance of escaping injury than one riding loose in the car should an accident occur or an emergency arise. If you do permit your dog to ride loose, never allow him to hang out a window, ears blowing in the breeze. An injury to his eyes could occur in this manner. He could also become overly excited by something he sees and jump out, or he could lose his balance and fall out.

Never, ever under any circumstances, should a dog be permitted to ride loose in the back of a pick-up truck. I have noted, with horror, that some people do transport dogs in this manner, and I think it cruel and shocking. How easily such a dog can be thrown out of the truck by sudden jolts or an impact! And I am sure that many dogs have jumped out at the sight of something exciting along the way. Some unthinking individuals tie the dog, probably not realizing that were he to jump under those circumstances, his neck would be broken, he could be dragged alongside the vehicle, or he could be hit by another vehicle. If you are for any reason taking your dog in an open back truck, please have sufficient regard for that dog to at least provide a crate for him, and then remember that, in or out of a crate, a dog riding under the direct rays of the sun in hot weather can suffer and have his life endangered by the heat.

If you are staying at a hotel or motel with your dog, exercise him somewhere other than in the flower beds and parking lot of the property. People walking to and from their cars really are not thrilled at "stepping in something" left by your dog. Should an accident occur, pick it up with a tissue or a paper towel and deposit it in a proper receptacle; do not just walk off leaving it to remain there. Usually there are grassy areas on the sides of and behind motels where dogs can be exercised. Use them rather than the more conspicuous, usually carefully tended, front areas or those close to the rooms. If you are becoming a dog show enthusiast, you will eventually need an exercise pen to take with you to the show. Exercise pens are ideal to use when staying at motels, too, as they permit you to limit the dog's roaming space and to pick up after him more easily.

Never leave your dog unattended in the room of a motel unless you are absolutely, positively certain that he will stay there quietly and not damage or destroy anything. You do not want a long list of complaints from irate guests, caused by the annoying barking or whining of a lonesome dog in strange surroundings or an overzealous watch dog barking furiously each time a footstep passes the door or he hears a sound from an adjoining room. And you certainly do not want to return to torn curtains or bedspreads, soiled rugs, or other embarrassing evidence of the fact that your dog is not really house-reliable after all.

If yours is a dog accustomed to travelling with you and you are positive that his behavior will be acceptable when left alone, that is fine. But if the slightest uncertainty exists, the wise course is to leave him in the car while you go to dinner or elsewhere; then bring him into the room when you are ready to retire for the night.

When you travel with a dog, it is often simpler to take along from home the food and water he will need rather than buying food and looking for water while you travel. In this way he will have the rations to which he is accustomed and which you know agree with him, and there will be no fear of problems due to different drinking water. Feeding on the road is quite easy now, at least for short trips, with all the splendid dry prepared foods and high-quality canned meats available. A variety of lightweight, refillable water containers can be bought at many types of stores.

Daryl Martin as a youngster earned wide acclaim with Rena Martin's gorgeous brace, Ch. Martin's Jingles Puff and Ch. Martin's Bangles Puff. Here they are winning Best Brace in Show at Lake Minnetonka in 1969.

If you are going to another country, you will need a health certificate from your veterinarian for each dog you are taking with you, certifying that each has had rabies shots within the required time preceding your visit.

Be careful always to leave sufficient openings to ventilate your car when the dog will be alone in it. Remember that during the summer, the rays of the sun can make an inferno of a closed car within only a few minutes, so leave enough window space open to provide air circulation. Again, if your dog is in a crate, this can be done quite safely. The fact that you have left the car in a shady spot is not always a guarantee that you will find conditions the same when you return. Don't forget that the position of the sun changes in a matter of minutes, and the car you left nicely shaded half an hour ago can be getting full sunlight far more quickly than you may realize. So, if you leave a dog in the car, make sure there is sufficient ventilation and check back frequently to ascertain that all is well.

Ch. Gordon's Legend of Russ Ann, owned by Pauline Clarke, has several Group wins to his credit and is now residing in Switzerland with Jacques and Renate Aubort. He completed his Swiss Championship and his International Championship. Bred by Anna Mae Hardy, "Rusty" is a son of Ch. C. and M's Valentino of Midhill from Ch. Russ Ann Petite Charmer.

Chapter XIV
Responsibilities of
Breeders and Owners

The first responsibility of any person breeding dogs is to do so with care, forethought, and deliberation. It is inexcusable to breed more litters than you need to carry on your show program or to perpetuate your bloodlines. A responsible breeder should not cause a litter to be born without definite plans for the safe and happy disposition of the puppies.

A responsible dog breeder makes absolutely certain, so far as is humanly possible, that the home to which one of his puppies will go is a good home, one that offers proper care and an enthusiastic owner. I have tremendous admiration for those people who insist on visiting (although doing so is not always feasible) the prospective owners of their puppies, to see if they have suitable facilities for keeping a dog, that they understand the responsibility involved, and that all members of the household are in accord regarding the desirability of owning one. All breeders should carefully check out the credentials of prospective purchasers to be sure that the puppy is being placed in responsible hands.

I am certain that no breeder ever wants a puppy or grown dog he has raised to wind up in an animal shelter, in an experimental laboratory, or as a victim of a speeding car. While complete control of such a situation may be impossible, it is at least our responsibility to make every effort to turn over dogs to responsible people. When selling a puppy, it is a good idea to do so with the understanding that should it become necessary to place the dog in other hands, the purchaser will first contact you, the breeder. You may want to help in some way, possibly by buying or taking back the dog or placing it elsewhere. It is not fair just to sell our puppies and then never again give a thought to their welfare. Family problems arise, people may be forced to move where dogs are prohibited, or people just plain grow bored with a dog and its care. Thus the dog becomes a victim. You, as the dog's breeder, should concern yourself with the welfare of each of your dogs and see to it that the dog remains in good hands.

The final obligation every dog owner shares, be there just one dog or an entire kennel involved, is that of making detailed, explicit plans for the future of our dearly loved animals in the event of the owner's death. Far too many of us are apt to procrastinate and leave this very important matter unattended to, feeling that everything will work out or that "someone will see to them." The latter is not too likely, at least not to the benefit of the dogs, unless you have done some advance planning which will assure their future well-being.

Life is filled with the unexpected, and even the youngest, healthiest, most robust of us may be the victim of a fatal accident or sudden illness. The fate of our dogs, so entirely in our hands, should never be left to chance. If you have not already done so, please get together with your lawyer and set up a clause in your will specifying what you want done with each of your dogs, to whom they will be entrusted (after first making absolutely certain that the person selected is willing and able to assume the responsibility), and telling the locations of all registration papers, pedigrees, and kennel records. Just think of the possibilities which might happen otherwise! If there is another family member who shares your love of the dogs, that is good and you have less to worry about. But if your heirs are not dog-oriented, they will hardly know how to proceed or how to cope with the dogs themselves, and they may wind up disposing of or caring for your dogs in a manner that would break your heart were you around to know about it.

In our family, we have specific instructions in each of our wills for each of our dogs. A friend, also a dog person who regards her own dogs with the same concern and esteem as we do ours, has agreed to take over their care until they can be placed accordingly and will make certain that all will work out as we have planned. We have this person's name and phone number prominently displayed in our van and car and in our wallets. Our lawyer is aware of this fact. It is all spelled out in our wills. The friend has a signed check of ours to be used in case of an emergency or accident when we are travelling with the dogs; this check will be us-

Ch. Martin's Chanel-Cid showing head with slight profile. Marjorie Martin bred, owns and photographed this exquisite Maltese. Martin's Maltese are at Columbus, Ohio.

At the start of her winning career, Ch. Co Ca He's Aennchen's Toy Dancer, "Toya" to her friends, won a strong group at Trenton Kennel Club in May 1963. Handled by Richard Bauer for owner Anna Marie Stimmler. Anna K. Nicholas, judge.

ed to cover her expense to come and take over the care of our dogs should anything happen to make it impossible for us to do so. This, we feel, is the least any dog owner should do in preparation for the time our dogs suddenly find themselves without us. There have been so many sad cases of dogs unprovided for by their loving owners, left to heirs who couldn't care less and who disposed of them in any way at all to get rid of them, or left to heirs who kept and neglected them under the misguided idea that they were providing them "a fine home with lots of freedom." All of us *must* prevent any of these misfortunes befalling our own dogs who have meant so much to us!

Index